T0354736

BOOKS BY JAY R. LEACH (Pen name Jay Leach)

How Should We Then Live
Behold the Man
The Blood Runs Through It
Drawn Away
Give Me Jesus
A Lamp unto My Feet
Grace that Saves
The Narrow Way
Radical Restoration in the Church
Manifestation of the True Children of God
According to Pattern
Battle Cry
Is there not a Cause?
We would See Jesus
According to Pattern 2nd Edition
The Apostolic Rising
For His Glory
Where have all the Shepherds Gone?
Out of Babylon
Living Grace 24/7
When God's Command becomes A Question
It Is Finished

IT IS FINISHED

I CAN DO ALL THINGS THROUGH CHRIST

JAY LEACH

ISBN: 978-1-6987-1747-0 (sc)
ISBN: 978-1-6987-1748-7 (e)

Trafford rev.   08/17/2024

 www.trafford.com
North America & international
toll-free: 844-688-6899 (USA & Canada)
fax: 812 355 4082

CONTENTS

SECTION ONE
Get The Real Thing

Chapter 1   The Blood And The Cross 1
Chapter 2   Knowing ... This 11
Chapter 3   Your Faith Must Be Visible 18
Chapter 4   This Is That 28

SECTION TWO
The Spirit-Word In Tandem

Chapter 5   Don't Divorce The Holy Spirit 39
Chapter 6   Spirit And Word 43
Chapter 7   Don't Be Fooled 50
Chapter 8   The Wrath Of God 63

SECTION THREE
Get Right Or Get Left

Chapter 9   Biblical Discipleship Is Not Optional 73
Chapter 10   Why Is Disciple-Making Ignored In The Local Church? 82
Chapter 11   It Takes A Disciple To Make A Disciple 91
Chapter 12   Shake The Dust Off Your Feet 97

SECTION FOUR
Winning Souls For Christ

Chapter 13 Winning Tomorrow's World Today 107
Chapter 14 A Mature Person In Christ............................. 117
Chapter 15 Our Walk With Christ 122
Chapter 16 Walking In Victory...................................... 135
Chapter 17 The Christian Soldier's Charge!................... 141
Chapter 18 The Wiles, Devices, And Deceptions Of The Devil....... 146

DEDICATION

For all of our grands and great grandchildren 16 of God's greatest gifts.

There is much your grandmother, and I can teach you, but none of it matters more than what's in this book.

DEDICATION

INTRODUCTION

This book is for all gospel believing Christians living on purpose. Its object is to show that true Christian life is something far different from the life of the average Christian today. Through social media and other sources many people place their faith in a *false gospel* and still identify themselves as Christians. In the pages of this book you will find an overview of the crumbling foundations of Christianity, and how the Biblical Christian Worldview of our Christian churches are eroded or totally rejected. Also you will observe how Christians can not only see it, but counter it with the truth of God's Word! It has been said, "America is the land of the over-churched and under-reached" and churches must understand that *everything* from church membership criteria, holiday services, Vacation Bible School, anniversary celebrations, and other typical traditional programming of the American local church can either promote cultural Christianity, or cripple it and bring it down. Throughout this book, we'll come back to the *simple principle* – that true gospel clarity is the antidote to the rampart confusion of the so-called "new worldview": the gospel shows that God makes the demands, meets them in Christ, and then calls people to trust in and follow Him. There's an old saying that says, "When all else fail, follow instructions!" The Bible is the most *basic* and *relevant* book in the world. If we would consider the Bible, [which is the written Word of God], and the Sermon on the Mount for example – should lead us to ask if such a life has ever in fact been lived on the earth, except [only by the Son of God Himself]. Only in the last seven words of the second clause do we find the answer to our question.

The apostle Paul shares his own definition of that (Christian) life.[1] *"It is no longer I, but Christ."* So, we believe, presenting God's normal for a Christian, can be summarized, "I no longer live, but Christ lives His life in me." God has made it clear in His Word that He has only one answer for *every* human need – His Son, Jesus Christ. You may be asking "only one?" Only One! He works by first taking us out of the way and substituting Christ in our place. The Son of God <u>died instead of us for our forgiveness [HIS BLOOD], and He lives (HIS LIFE within us by the HOLY SPIRIT) which He has given to us for our deliverance [VICTORY]</u>.

It will help us tremendously, and save us from much confusion, if we constantly keep before us this fact, that God will answer all our questions in one way and only one way, namely, by showing us more of His Son. Do not be lulled to sleep because of a good reputation. Keep pressing unto Jesus. Make sure you practice the teachings you have received; and continue to receive through His Word. Being ready to repent for any failure, to make right any sin, will cause gospel believers to refine their walk in the Spirit. Outward works do not always indicate the right condition of the heart, but a right condition of the heart produces good works. Further, the primary purpose of this book is to call Christians to action, especially pastors, and Bible teachers who realize they have inadvertently allowed the culture's "New Worldview" to go unchallenged in their local churches. May this book point us to Jesus Christ, so that we can remain humble and wise. None of what follows is intended to disparage falsely assured believers but rather to bring to light the great mission field before us and caution fellow Christians to get serious about the gospel of Jesus Christ and proclaim this good news unapologetically. Truly, it is the **power of God** for salvation to all who would believe! Only the indwelling Holy Spirit can fulfill the Law through us, reproduce the dynamic life of Christ in us, and truly free us from the Law. Obey God's Word to you!

---

[1]   Galatians 2:20

I have added a study guide at the end of each chapter; to help reinforce and stabilize your daily Christian Walk with God; and Biblical Worldview while applying these truths of His Word.

Jay Leach, pastor, Bible teacher, author
Fayetteville, NC

SECTION ONE

GET
THE REAL
THING

CHAPTER ONE

The Blood And The Cross

"I have been crucified with Christ; it is no longer I who live, but Christ lives in me. And the life which I now live in the flesh I live by faith in the Son of God, who loved me and gave Himself for me." (Galatians 2:20 ESV)

The apostle Paul gives us his own definition of the life of the Christian. *"It is no longer I, but Christ."* He is not stating something special, or a higher level of Christianity. He is simply presenting God's Spiritual life for a Christian – I no longer live, but Christ lives *His life in and through me.* God has made it perfectly clear in His Word that He has only one answer to *every* human need – His Son, Jesus Christ.

In all of His dealings with us God works by taking (self) us out of the way and substituting Christ in our place – our biblical, Christian Worldview.

1

THE WAY OF SALVATION AND DELIVERANCE

Paul proceeds then to set forth the way of salvation which is not the way of obedience to the law. The law awakens man to his condition and thus makes his salvation possible, but it is powerless to *deliver* him from the bondage of sin or to save him from corruption and death.

This deliverance and salvation have been accomplished not through the law, but through Jesus Christ. "God has done what the law ... could not do: sending His own Son in the likeness of flesh and for sin, He condemned sin in in the flesh [i.e., placed it under sentence of death]" (Romans 8:3; also see Acts 13:39; Isaiah 53:11). Emphasis added.

It is the way of *justification* [in response to faith in Jesus Christ]. Often expressed in teaching to define justification as "just as if I have never sinned."

DEALING WITH SINS AND SIN

Paul points out a situation in the first eight chapters of the Book of Romans often called ["the fifth gospel"]. There is a natural division which is often overlooked by those churches who do not disciple their people. A verse by verse reading of this section reveals that we are actually dealing with two subjects. From chapter 1 to 5:11 we deal with the plural *"sins"* a clear matter of how many sins I have committed before God. However, in the second it is a question of *sin as a principle* working in me. Therefore, in the second section Romans 5:12 to 8:39, we see this changed and the singular word "sin" is dominate. Why is that? Because no matter how many sins I commit – it is always the one *sin principle* working in me that leads to them. I need forgiveness for my sins – but I need deliverance from the power of sin.

I need forgiveness for what I have done – but I need deliverance from what I am!

GOD'S REMEDY FOR BOTH: THE BLOOD AND THE CROSS

In the first part of Romans 1 to 8, we find two references to the Blood of the Lord Jesus, in chapter 3:25 and in chapter 5:9. In the second, a new idea is introduced in chapter 6:6 where we are said to have been "crucified" with Christ. The argument of part one centers now around that aspect of the work of the Lord Jesus which is represented by "the Blood" shed for our justification through the remission of sins.

Unlike the first part, this second part, where the argument centers now in the aspect of His work represented by "the Cross," that means by our union with Christ in His death, burial, and resurrection.[2] This a very important! We shall see that the Blood deals with what we have done – whereas the Cross deals with what we are. The Blood washes away our sins, while the Cross strikes at the *root* of our capacity to sin.

When God's light of salvation comes in my heart my one cry is for forgiveness, for I realize I have committed sins before Him; but once I have received forgiveness of my sins, I make a new discovery, namely, the discovery of sin, and I realize not only that I have committed sins before God but that there is something wrong within me. I discover that I have a *sinful nature*. There is an inward inclination to sin, a power within that draws you to sin. When that power breaks out I commit sins. I may seek and receive forgiveness, but then I sin once more. So life goes on in a vicious circle of sinning and begging for forgiveness and then sinning again. I appreciate the blessed fact of God's forgiveness, but I want something more than that: I want *deliverance*. I need forgiveness for what I have done, but I need also deliverance from what I am.

We have seen that Romans 1 to 8 falls into two sections, in the first of which are shown that the Blood deals with what we have done – later in the second we shall see that the Cross deals with *what we are*. Again, we need the Blood for forgiveness; we need also the Cross for deliverance.

THE PRECIOUS BLOOD JESUS

We begin, then, with the precious Blood of the Lord Jesus Christ and its value to each of us in dealing with our sins and justifying us in the sight of God. Note the following passages:

---

[2]   The Gospel of Christ 1 Corinthians 15:1-4

All have sinned and fall short of the glory of God. (Romans 3:23 NKJV)

But God demonstrates His own love toward us, in that while we were still sinners, Christ died for us. Much more then, having now been justified by His blood, we shall be saved from wrath through Him. (Romans 5:8, 9 NKJV)

Being justified freely by His grace through the redemption that is in Christ Jesus, who is set forth to be a propitiation, by His blood, through faith, to demonstrate His righteousness, because in His forbearance God had passed over the sins that were previously committed, to demonstrate at the present time His righteousness, that He might be just and the justifier of the one who has faith in Jesus Christ. (Romans 3:24-26 NKJV)

The conclusion is the whole world is guilty before God because "no flesh" is justified by the deeds of the flesh. (see Romans 3:20). Judged by their own merits, as to their deeds, Gentile and Jew alike are guilty. This is the end of the matter. God has spoken, and He is the righteous Judge of the whole world. God did not give the Law to save men. The Law never will save anyone. For by the Law is the knowledge of sin. If you want to know the truth concerning Christianity and the Law, you can read and learn the truth in Romans 10:4: *"For Christ is the end of the Law for righteousness to everyone that beliveth."* Please note, this does not mean that Jesus ended the Law. In Matthew 5:17 Jesus tells us that He did not come to destroy the Law, nor the prophets. He came to fulfill the Law – and that He did. He satisfied the demands of God's holiness and purity. At the close of His earthly ministry He said, *"I HAVE FINISHED THE WORK WHICH THOU GAVEST ME TO DO."* (John 17:4 KJV). Just before He bowed His head on His breast. He cried out from the cross. *"IT IS FINISHED!"*(John 19:30 KJV)

God has not changed His mind about the Law. He loudly says, ***"The soul that sinneth, it shall die!"*** (Ezekiel 18:20 KJV) God said that, and He means exactly what He said, *but Jesus took our place!* Today, living in this Dispensation of Grace, when God looks at the believer, He sees the precious blood of Jesus that covers our heart. In Christ we are holy. Out of Christ we are helpless, and hopeless. Please study the following passages:

> "That no flesh should glory in His presence. But of Him you are in Christ Jesus, who became for us wisdom from God – and righteousness and sanctification and redemption." (I Corinthians 1:29, 30 NKJV)

> "For He made Him who knew no sin to be sin for us, that we might become the righteousness of God in Him." (II Corinthians 5:21 NKJV)

Again, Jesus did for us what we never could have done for ourselves. In fact, Jesus did for us what man *would never have done for himself,* even *if he could have.* Please note: "He came unto His own, and His own received Him not. But as many as received Him, to them he gave the power to become the sons of God, even to them that believe on His name: Which were born, NOT OF BLOOD, NOR OF THE WILL OF MAN, BUT OF GOD!" (John 1:11-13 KJV) Emphasis added.

In verse 12 of this passage of Scripture; that God gives the power. God furnishes the power when we believe; but *"how shall they believe in Him of whom they have not heard? And how shall they hear without a preacher? And how shall they preach, except they be sent?"* (Please read carefully Romans 10:13-17).

God sent the Word down to us in Jesus – the Word of God *in flesh* (see John 1:1, 14). We hear the Gospel (1 Corinthians 15:1-4). The Gospel convicts of sin; the Gospel draws men to God. Therefore, we receive new birth into God's family through the power of the Gospel (see Romans 1:16).

We do not become a Child of God through man's blood, no matter the pedigree. We do not become a child of God through the will of the flesh, we do not become a child of God through the will of man ... "but of God." No man except Jesus has ever been willing to do exactly and all that God commanded. We remember that in the Garden of Gethsemane when Jesus saw "the cup" He prayed, "Father, if it be possible, let this cup pass. Nevertheless, **not My will, but thine be done.**" Jesus is the only

Man who ever satisfied God. He is the only Man who was ever willing for God to command every minute detail of His life, His words, and His actions.

Jesus did in the flesh what the Law never could have done, what man never could have done. Adam, Noah, Abraham, Moses, and David ... all men have failed God; but Jesus willingly took our place and paid sin's debt. He paid the ransom note, and we can go free if we believe in Him who took our place. So we see that objectively the Blood deals with *our sins*. The Lord Jesus has borne them on the Cross for us as our Substitute and has thereby obtained for us forgiveness, justification, and reconciliation. But we must now go a step further in the plan of God to understand how He deals with *the sin principle within us*. [**This is Important!**] especially for those churches that do not disciple their people.

MY OLD MAN

The Blood can wash away my sins, but it cannot wash away "my old man." It needs the *Cross to crucify me*. The Blood deals with the *sins* – but the Cross deals with the *sinner*. You will only find the word "sinner" mentioned a few times in the first four chapters of Romans. The reason being, the sinner himself is not mainly in view, but rather the sins he or she has committed. The word "sinner" becomes prominent only in chapter 5. In that chapter a sinner is said to be sinner because he or she is born a sinner; not because he or she has committed sins. [**This distinction is important!**] Often, we have begun our witnessing to others citing Romans 3:23, where it says, "all have sinned." This could lead a person to believe that we are sinners because we commit sins – rather than *we sin because we are sinners*. We are sinners by birth rather than by action. As Romans 5:19 says it: *"For as by one man's disobedience many were **made** sinners.*

How were we made sinners? By Adam's disobedience. We do not become sinners by what we have done but what Adam has done and has become. So chapter 3 draws our attention to what we have done – all have sinned – but again, it is not because we have done it that we become sinners. Yes, one who sins is a sinner, but the fact that he or she sins is merely the evidence that they are already sinners – it is not a cause. One who sins is a sinner, but it is equally true of the one who does not sin, if he or she is Adam's descendant is a sinner to, and in need of redemption. Are you with me? We are sinners, not because of ourselves but because I was in Adam when he sinned.

We derive our existence from Adam, and because his life became a sinful life, and *sinful nature,* therefore the nature which we receive from him is sinful also. So as we said earlier, the trouble is in our heredity, not in our behavior. Unless we can change our parentage there is no *deliverance for us.* **But** it is in this very direction that God has dealt with us.

AS IN ADAM SO IN CHRIST

In Romans 5:12-21 we are told the story of Adam and the sin principle in an impossible situation [we can't change our parentage]. However we also see that God's plan is moving on through the Lord Jesus. As through the one man's *disobedience* the many were *made sinners* – even so through the *obedience* of the One shall the many be *made righteous. In* Adam we receive everything that is of Adam: *in* Christ we receive everything that is of Christ.

So we are presented with a *new* solution. In Adam all is lost. Through the disobedience of one man we were all made sinners. By him sin entered and death through sin, and throughout all humanity sin has reigned unto death from that day on. But Praise be to God! through the obedience of Another we may be made righteous. Where sin abounded grace did much more abound, and as sin reigned unto death, even so may grace reign through righteousness into eternal life by Jesus Christ our Lord (see Romans 5:19-21). Our despair is in Adam; our hope is in Christ.

DEVINE DELIVERANCE

It is God's clear plan that this should lead to our *practical deliverance from sin.* Paul makes this quite clear as he opens chapter 6 of his Roman letter with the question: *"Shall[3] we continue in sin?"* His whole being rejects even the very thought. Certainly not! *How shall we who died to*

---

[3]   Webster's New Student dictionary. "Shall" here is used to express a command or exhortation (you shall go). Used in laws, regulations, or directives (to express what is mandatory (it shall be unlawful to carry firearms).

sin live any longer in it? Or do you not know that as many of us as were *baptized into Christ Jesus were baptized into His death? Therefore we were buried with Him through baptism into death, that just as Christ was raised from the dead by the glory of the Father, even so we also should walk in newness of life* (v. 4) Emphasis mine.

How did you receive forgiveness? You realized that the Lord Jesus died as your substitute and bore your sins upon Himself, and that His Blood was shed to cleanse away your defilement. What is true for your *forgiveness* is also true for your *deliverance*. Do you believe that the Lord Jesus died? **[this is important!]** God has put us in Christ, so that when Christ was crucified, we were crucified also. Therefore, the work is done! You do not need to pray about your sins, your sins were dealt with, but you praise Him for it! You were dealt with at the Cross, when Christ was crucified so where we. Praise Him for it! Again, I was crucified when Christ was crucified and I died when He died, because I was in Him. He not only died in my place, but He bore me with Him to the Cross, so that when He died, I also died. And if I believe in the death of the Lord Jesus, then I can believe in my own *death* just as surely as I can believe in His *death*.

Why do you believe that the Lord Jesus died? Is it because you *feel* He has died? No! You believe it because the Word of God has said it. It does not depend on your feelings. When Jesus was crucified, two thieves were crucified at the same time but on different crosses. You do not doubt that they were crucified with Him either, because the Scripture plainly says so. These are divine facts. That you have died is a fact also. You are out. That old man (that you hate) is on the Cross in Christ. "And he that is dead is freed from sin." (Romans 6:7 NASB) This is the Gospel for Christians. Our crucifixion can never be made effective by your will or effort – but by accepting what the Lord Jesus did on the Cross. Many today have tried to save themselves. They try to read the Bible, pray, go to church, and tithe their income. I pray that their eyes will be opened and see that a full salvation has already been provided for you on the Cross. You are offered deliverance from *sin* as no less gift of God's grace than was the forgiveness of your *sins*.

God sets us free from the dominion of sin, not by strengthening our "old man" but by crucifying him; not by helping him to do anything but by removing him from the scene of action. Praise God!

Perhaps for years, you have tried fruitlessly to exercise control over yourself, and maybe this is still your experience; but when you see the truth you will recognize that you are actually powerless to do anything, but in setting aside altogether God has done it all. Such a discovery brings human striving and self-effort to an end.

This is a shortfall in the lives and walks of many Christians. God's means of delivering us from sin is not by making us *weaker* and *weaker.* Certainly that is a peculiar way to victory you may say – but it is God's way! God sets us free from dominion of sin, not by strengthening our "old man" but by crucifying him; not by helping him to do anything but by removing him from the scene of action. When we believe on the Lord Jesus Christ from the heart unto salvation, we experience all that He experienced. By that I mean *we die to the world,* and we are given new life in Him. True believers are in Christ, and Christ is in the true believer. Let's layout what Paul is clearly teaching here:

- That no one can share in Christ's resurrection except he or she first die.
- That the resurrection to a new life in Christ is the result of dying to the world with Him.
- That we are buried in order to be raised (John 12:24).
- That Paul clearly reveals the union between the believer and Christ – for the thought is, if we have gone into the baptism in union, why should we not come out in union?

STUDY GUIDE: CHAPTER 1
THE BLOOD AND THE CROSS

1. The apostle Paul gave his definition of the life of a Christian,
   "_____ _____ _____ _____ _____
   _____ _____."

2. Deliverance and salvation have been accomplished through
   _____ _____.

3. There is a natural division in the first eight chapters of Romans:
   Chapters 1-5 deals with "_____" and 5:12-8:39 deals
   with _____.

4. The blood of Jesus deals with _____ _____
   _____ _____.

5. The cross of Jesus deals with _____
   _____ _____.

6. We need the blood for _____ and we need the _____
   for _____.

7. We were made sinners by Adam's _____.

CHAPTER TWO

Knowing ... This

"Knowing this, that our old man was crucified with Him, that the body of sin might be done away with, that we should no longer be slaves of sin." (Romans 6:6 NKJV)

"Our old man" is our old selves before we were saved, contrasted with the "new man," which is what we are and have *in* Christ. The apostle Paul uses this same expression in Ephesians 4:22 and Colossians 3:9. The words "our old man is *crucified*" are addressed to faith. In Galatians 2:20 the same proclamation is repeated:

> *"I am crucified with Christ: nevertheless I live; yet not I, but Christ liveth in me: and the life which I now live in the flesh I live by faith of the Son of God, who loved me, and gave Himself for me." (KJV) Emphasis added.*

As is our theme throughout Paul is saying, "I died when Jesus died on the cross." When Jesus hung on the cross, the passersby saw only *one Man dying* on that cross; but God, the Father saw *more* than one Man.

God saw more than a physical body. God saw the *spiritual body,* the mystical body of Christ [the Church of the Living God]. By grace Paul was in Christ as He hung on the cross, and what happened to Jesus on the cross happened to Paul, since he was in Christ. What happened to Paul happened to every born-again believer from then until the Church is completed and caught up to meet Jesus in the air.

LET'S BE CLEAR

Let us be clear, the "old man" and the "flesh" are not the same. The Flesh has not changed – and we must not confuse them. Knowing this, that our old man was crucified with Him. Notice, the tense of the verb is very important, for it puts the event right back there in the past. The thing has been done and can never be undone. Our old man has been crucified once and can never be uncrucified. This is what we need to know. Then, when we know this, what follows? The next command is in verse 11. "Likewise, "reckon ye" also yourselves to be dead indeed unto sin, but alive unto God through Jusus Christ our Lord." (KJV). Often, when presenting the truth of our union with Christ the emphasis has more frequently been placed on this second matter of reckoning ourselves to be dead, as if that was the starting point, however, it should be based on divine revelation knowledge. When we know that our old man has been crucified with Christ, then the next step is to "reckon it so."

People are always trying to reckon without knowledge. Reckoning and faith here are practically the same thing. The first-and-a-half chapters of Romans speak of faith. We are *justified* by *faith* in Him (see Romans 3:28).

Righteousness, the forgiveness of our sins, and peace with God are all ours *by faith,* and without faith in the finished work of Jesus Christ *none* can possess them. Faith is my acceptance of God's truths. It always has its foundations in the past.

What relates to the to the future is hope rather than faith, although faith often has its object or goal in the future, as in Hebrews 11. What then is the secret of reckoning? In one word it is revelation. We need revelation from God Himself:

> Jesus answered and said to him, *"Blesses are you, Simon Bar-Jonah, for flesh and blood has not revealed this to you, but My Father which is in heaven."*(Matthew 16:17-18 NKJV)

THE KNOWLEDGE OF GOD

> *"That the God of our Lord Jesus Christ, the Father of glory, may give to you the spirit of wisdom and revelation in the knowledge of Him."* (Ephesians 1:17-18 NKJV)

We are living in a day of horrifying ignorance that nothing can be taken for granted. Therefore, we need to point out that in asking God for these particular things Paul did not signify the Ephesians were totally devoid of them any more than his opening *"grace be unto you and peace"* (Ephesians 1:2) implied they possessed neither the one nor the other; rather he desired for them an increase of both. Thus it is here. They already had a saving knowledge of God or he would not have addressed them as "saints" and *"faithful in Christ Jesus"* (Eph. 1:1). In asking God to grant them the *"Spirit of wisdom* and *revelation,"* though this was not the first time of this request, for he had just affirmed in the context that they were *"sealed with the Holy Spirit of promise"* (Eph. 1:13). Rather he was making a request for them for further supplies and a richer outpouring of the Holy Spirit upon them. Paul prayed for a fuller, deeper, closer relationship with Him, and "increasing in the knowledge of God" as Colossians 1:10 expresses it.

Our eyes need to be open to the truth of our union with Christ, and that is something more than knowing it as a doctrine. What is meant by the *"knowledge of Him?"* As we find more than one kind of faith in the Scripture, so there are several different varieties of "knowledge" – not only of different objects and subjects known but of ways of knowing them. One may know or be fully assured from the testimony of reliable witnesses that fire produces unpleasant effects if an unprotected hand is pushed into it.

But if I have *personally* felt the consequences of being burned, I have quite a different order of knowledge. The one may be termed theoretical, or imaginary, the other experiential – sometimes wrongfully termed "experimental." The distinction frequently drawn between *real* and *assumed* knowledge does not define the difference. When the unclean spirit said to Jesus, "I know thee who thou art" (Mark 1:24 KJV), his knowledge was both *real* and *accurate,* but it profited him nothing spiritually. In other words, *"they that know thy name will put their trust in thee"* (Psalm 9:10) speaks of a knowledge which inspires such assurance that its possessor cannot help but believe. This is important.

As there are degrees of trusting God, so there are degrees in our knowledge of Him, and the measure in which we *know* Him will determine the extent to which we *love, trust,* and *obey* Him. Since that's the way it is, we may at once perceive the vital importance of obtaining a *fuller knowledge* of God. The defectiveness of our faith, love, and obedience is traced to the inadequacy of our knowledge of God. If we were more intimately and influentially acquainted with Him, we would:

- Love Him more fervently
- Trust Him more implicitly
- Obey Him more freely

We cannot adequately realize the value of a better knowledge of God. But I say again, it is not a mere imaginary knowledge of Him but a visual and vital one that is needed. The first kind is one in which ideas or mental images are presented to the understanding to work on, but secondly, it brings the reality of them down in the *heart.* By such knowledge we behold the glory of the Lord and *"are changed into the same image"* (2 Corinthians 3:18).

The "old man" is all that we are (in Adam) before we are "born again" contrasted with the "new man" which is all that we are and have in Christ.

In the passage above the reference to the "body" is therefore to the believer's *physical body before salvation,* possessed by or dominated and controlled by the *sinful nature.* That is, what the believer was before he or she was saved. Now we are crucified with Christ in order that our physical body which before salvation was dominated by a sinful nature, might be *rendered inoperative* in that respect, in that of being controlled by the *sinful nature,* in order that no longer are we rendering a *habitual obedience* to the sinful nature as before salvation. "Knowing this," says Paul, that our old man was crucified with him, that the body of sin might be done away, that so, we should no longer be in bondage to sin. (see Romans 6:6)

God is not out to reform our lives. He has no plan to bring that life to a certain level of refinement, for it is totally on the wrong level. On that level, God cannot bring *man* to glory. He must have a *new man;* one born of God. Regeneration and justification go together.

When we believe on the Lord Jesus Christ, we become a new man. We are regenerated, and [a regenerated person is to be distinguished from a person who has never been saved]. As a new man we *"become partaker of divine nature and divine life"* (see II Peter 1:4; Colossians 3:3-4).

Here the fact is stated that this disengagement of the believer from the evil nature has been brought about by God. Such revelation is no vague thing. Most of us can remember the day when we saw clearly *that Christ died for us,* and we ought to be equally conscious as to the time when we saw that *we died with Christ.* It should not be hazy but extremely definite – for this is the basis for our going on.

The Bible does not teach that the "old man" is made over or improved, or as we would say, "overhauled." (Carefully study 2 Corinthians 5:17; Galatians 6:15; Ephesians 2:10; and Colossians 3:10)

DELIVERANCE FROM SIN'S POWER

Should we who name the name of Jesus, who profess to be followers of Christ continue sinning that *grace* may abound? Paul exclaimed, "God forbid." We who are born again into the family of God have died out of the family of the devil. We as Christians have shared Christ's death, and in sharing Christ's death, we died to sin. We were by nature the children of the devil, but upon receiving the Lord Jesus Christ we were translated out of the kingdom of darkness "into the kingdom of His dear Son"(see Colossians 1:13).

We who are believers have been *raised* from the deadness of sin and planted by the *power of the Holy Spirit* into the body of Christ. God forbid that we continue in sin. How shall we that are dead to sin, live any longer therein?" Having said earlier that revelation leads spontaneously to reckoning we *must not* lose sight of the fact that we are presented with a command: "Reckon ye …" There is a definite *attitude* for us to take. How is this all possible? In Christ Jesus!

Never forget that it is always and only true *in Christ*. But it is a question of faith not in yourself but in Him! You look to the Lord and know what He has done. Lord, "I believe in you!"

STUDY GUIDE: CHAPTER 2 KNOWING ... THIS

1. Our "old man" is our _____ _____ before we were saved; and our "new man is our _____.

2. On the cross God saw more than a physical body; God saw the _____ body (the church of the Living God).

3. Our old man has been crucified _____ and without _____.

4. People are always trying to "reckon" without _____.

5. Should we who are in Christ _____ in sin, that _____ many abound?

6. As believers we have been raised from the deadness of sin and planted by the power of the _____ _____ into the _____ of _____.

7. There is a definite _____ we are to take.

CHAPTER THREE

Your Faith Must Be Visible

For as the body without the spirit is dead, so faith without works is dead also. (James 2:26 NKJV)

Yes, faith without works cannot be called faith. "Faith without works is dead," and a dead faith is worse than no faith at all. Faith that works must produce, and it must be visible. Verbal faith is not enough; mental faith is insufficient. I was raised in a Christian home by parents who loved and followed Jesus through 60 years of pastoral ministry – with their biblical Christian worldview. Through their example and leadership, God impressed upon me that he was well worth paying attention to.

After graduation from High School at age 18, I enlisted in the US Army, as a young Christian I paid more attention to the written rules of religion than I did to the life-giving divine relationship. Therefore, I embarked on a military career that spanned 26.5 years and retirement. As a frustrated, legalistic law-keeper who was far from God, ignorant of the way of Jesus Christ and unaware of the winsome fire of the Holy Spirit. After spending 1967-1968 in the Vietnam War and returning to my loving wife of five years and our three-year-old daughter, I immediately wanted the best for them; which meant the old life had to go!

Thankfully, God was not content with that life either. And he refused to leave me alone. Through joining my wife Magdalene and daughter at her home church; God showed me what a real, dynamic, and authentically human relationship with Jesus Christ could be. Through my wife and our new Christian friends, I saw what I had taken for granted in my faithful parents:

- They had a Biblical Christian worldview.
- They were *really* living the abundant life.
  And I wanted to live it too.

Like you, I have experienced much of what the world has to offer, truly it is not enough. For the first time, I became interested in the ways of God rather than just the laws of God. In our pursuit, God put many godly people in our path. He ignited a fire in me to speak His name out of an intimate relationship, not out of suggestion or religious obligation. Now, after 45 years of pastoring, and teaching the truth of God's Word, at 84 years old, I'm still excited about Christ and want all to receive Him in their hearts, especially as we near the end.

A doctrine I believe to be necessary in understanding our salvation *in Christ* is the "perseverance of the saints." To those who are *truly* born again – Jesus gave assurance concerning their salvation:

> *"This is the will of the Father who sent Me, that of all He has given Me I should lose nothing but should raise it up at the last day."* (John 6:39 NKJV)

If you believe that God's will is perfect and Jesus is perfect in carrying out the Father's will, then you know Jesus' *promise* that nobody is able to snatch His sheep out of the Father's hand (see John 10:28) is as true today as it was 2000 years ago. God has given salvation to those in Christ. Salvation is a gift, "eternal life that God, promised before time began" (see Titus 1:2). Salvation is based on work and promise, and that is not reserved for the moment of being born again, but also remaining "in Christ" until the end. The Christian can claim with the apostle Paul with confidence, "I am sure that He who started a good work in you will carry it on to completion until the day of Christ Jesus." (see Philippians 1:6).

MASS CONFUSION (FALSE ASSURANCE)

This wonderful biblical doctrine is meant to give the believer assurance and confidence in the *redemptive work of Christ* (see 1 Corinthians 15:1-4). However, many parents are caused to falsely think their children are eternally secure, because of the spin people put on this passage for various reasons. Also many claim salvation simply because of church attendance, which leads some parents to declare their children saved. Later as adults, false assurance keeps many from seeing their need of *evangelism* and *discipleship*. Overemphasizing a prayer can blind a person to the primary calls to salvation in the gospel (repentance, and faith). This is particularly dangerous for those who come forth in churches that do not disciple their people.

When Christian families admonish unbelieving relatives to "come back to church" the next step being practiced and preached is that the individual merely needs to get back to church with his or her family, or stop drinking so much, give up your friends, etc. While these are good goals, they must be motivated by genuine faith in Jesus Christ rather than familial expectations.

In dealing with these situations, we must prayerfully advance with a plan. It is possible that this family member grew up in church, asked Jesus to come into their heart, and was baptized. Yet, this person might be lost and in need of salvation; and the reality of being dead in sin must be addressed and acknowledged and he or she may be made alive in Christ (see Ephesians 2:1-4).

THE MARKS OF GENUINE CONVERSION

Surveys reflect that great numbers of people in the United States have prayed a sinner's prayer and think they're going to heaven because of it, even though there is no detectable difference in their lifestyles from those outside of the church. Therefore, many people are assured of *a* salvation that is hollow of the evidence of possessing on the basis of a prayer methods they didn't understand. At the same time so few hold orthodox views on topics including biblical inerrancy, salvation, and discipleship. This reality is that we need to preach salvation by *repentance* before God and *faith* in the finished work of Jesus Christ.

In the parable of the Sower, Jesus addressed those who never show any fruit of their claimed salvation. After telling the parable, He explained it to His disciples in detail:

> *"When anyone hears the word of the kingdom, and does not understand it, then the wicked one comes and snatches away what was sown in his heart. This is he who received seed by the wayside. "But he who received the seed on stoney places, this is he who hears the word and immediately receives it with joy; "yet he has no root in himself but endures only for a while. For when tribulation or persecution arises because of the word, immediately he stumbles. "Now he who received seed among the thorns is he who hears the word, and the cares of this world and the deceitfulness of riches choke the word, and he becomes unfruitful. "But he who received seed on the good ground is he who hears the word and understands it, who indeed bears fruit and produces; some a hundredfold, some sixty, some thirty."* (Matthew 13:19-23 NKJV)

Jesus gives us a standard for what true conversion looks like for the Christian:

1. Hear the word
2. Understand the word
3. Produce fruit.

Herein then are the evidence of genuine conversion. And let's not forget that this is possible *only* by grace, *not* human effort. Jesus called for fruit, and James declared that a life without it possesses no true faith at all (James 2:14). The Holy Spirit brings fruit and repentance, which stem from believing the gospel by faith.

LIFE OUT OF DEATH

> *"Most assuredly, I say to you, unless a grain of wheat falls into the ground and dies, it remains alone; but if it dies, it produces much grain."* (John 12:24 NKJV)

21

I consider this one of the most *essential* verses of Scripture a believer can embrace. Here the Lord Jesus Christ opens to you His relationship with the Father. But at the same time He goes on to show us something about who the Father is. The one thing our Father is, above all else: *He is a God with whom death is an essential to life.* The church of Jesus Christ must comprehend this truth:

DEATH IS AN ESSENTIAL PART OF THE LIFE OF GOD.

The death aspect of God is woven into the very nature of God: *All life will come out of death.* The message of the world and Satan, our enemy, is the opposite: "Do this and you will have life … do this and this and you will be better off than you are now." That was never the message of Jesus Christ. His message is, "only as you become *nothing* that you can possibly ever be anything." Once the church embraces this truth there can be true transformation.

It is on the cross that God magnified the true nature of His life. It was on the cross of Jesus Christ that we see the immovable principal that life comes *only* out of death. This is of spiritual significance. Sadly, the church today has quickly moved away from the message of the cross in the life of the believer. The cross is referred to at times in messages, but in practice, as seen in the very nature of God, Himself is virtually unknown.

An old illustration many of us have used: A young man walking through the city park he came upon a butterfly entangled in a cocoon, as he continued to watch the struggling butterfly, he decided to help it to break free. He picked up a stick and began to open up the cocoon. A voice behind shouted, "Don't TOUCH it!" It was too late, the butterfly fluttered to the ground and in a few seconds it was dead. The young man stood there in utter confusion asking. "Why?" The lady who shouted at him not to open the cocoon, explained, "The struggle the young butterfly was going through is a part of a process in which a worm spun itself into a cocoon and is through metamorphosis transformed into a butterfly, but in the struggle to break free of the cocoon the butterfly's wings are activated and strengthened. The cocoon falls off and the beautiful butterfly flies away. But you stopped the process. This is the case with many who would be converts. Again, this happens when a church does not disciple its people.

DO YOU CARRY A STICK?

God planted a number of trees in the Garden of Eden, but in the center, He planted two trees, the tree of life and the tree of the knowledge of good and evil. Visualize a man between 30 or 40 years old, who has no sense of right and wrong, and no power to differentiate between the two. I'm sure you would say that this man was *underdeveloped*. Well that was what Adam was. God brought him into the Garden of Eden and says to him in effect, "Now the garden is full of trees, full of fruits, and of the fruit of every tree you may eat freely. But in the very midst of the garden is one tree called "the tree of the knowledge of good and evil;" you must not eat of that tree – for in the day that you do so *you shall surly die*. But remember, the name of the other tree close by is *"Life."* What then was the significance of these two trees? Adam was created morally neutral – meaning neither sinful nor holy, but innocent. God put the two trees there so that he might exercise freewill. He could choose the tree of life, or he could choose the tree of the knowledge of good and evil.

Now the knowledge of good and evil, though forbidden to Adam, is not wrong in itself. Without it however, Adam is in a sense limited having been created innocent he cannot *decide for himself on moral issues.* Judgment of right and wrong does not reside in him – but in God. Adam's only course of action when faced with any question is to refer it to God. Thus, he was totally dependent on God. These two trees typify two deep principles – two levels of life, *the divine and the human.* The "tree of life" is God Himself, for God is life. He is the highest form or level of life, and also He is the source and goal of life. And the fruit is our Lord Jesus Christ. The fruit is the edible part, receivable part of the tree. So, may I humbly, and reverently, say, the Lord Jesus is really God in a receivable form. We can receive God in Christ.

1. If Adam chose the tree of life, he would partake of the life of God. Thus he would become a "son" of God, in the sense of having in him a life derived from God. There you would have God's life in union with man: a people having the life of God in them – and living in constant dependence *upon God for that life.*

2. But instead Adam turned the other way and took of the tree of the knowledge of good and evil, developing his own manhood along *natural lines* – apart from God. As a self-sufficient being, he possesses in himself the power to form independent judgment. But he would have no life from God.

3. So his alternative was choosing the way of the Spirit, the way of obedience, he could have become a "son" of God, living in dependence upon God for his life – he took the natural course putting the finishing touch to himself by becoming a self-dependent being, judging and acting *apart* from God. We are experiencing the *downward* outcome of the choice he made – worldwide today.

GOD IS NOT MOCKED

Adam chose the tree of the knowledge of good and evil, and thereby took up independent ground. In so doing he became as men are today in their own eyes [a fully developed man]. He could:

- command a knowledge,
- decide for himself
- go on or stop

From then on, he was wise (see Genesis 3:6). But the consequence for him **was still death rather than life,** because the choice he made involved *engaging* with Satan, and therefore, brought him under the judgment of God. That is why access to the tree of life had thereafter to be forbidden to him. Adam's choice was *sin*, because there he allied himself with Satan to destroy the eternal purpose of God. He did so by choosing to develop his manhood – to perhaps become a metropolitan man, and by his own standards perfect – all apart from God!

But the end was still death, because he did not have the divine life necessary to realize God's purpose in his being but had chosen instead to be an independent agent of the enemy. Therefore, in Adam we all become sinners, equally dominated by Satan, equally subject to the law of sin and death, and equally deserving of the wrath of God.

From this we see the divine reason for the *death and resurrection of the Lord Jesus.* Here we also see the reason for true consecration – for reckoning ourselves to be dead unto sin but alive unto God in Christ Jesus, and for presenting ourselves unto Him as alive from the dead. We must all go to the cross, because *what is in us by nature is self-life*, subject to the law of sin; so God had to gather up *all* that was in Adam and do away with it! Our "old man" has been crucified. God has put us all in Christ and crucified Him as the *last Adam*, and thus all that is of Adam has passed away. This is important!

CHRIST AROSE IN A NEW FORM

Then Christ arose in a new form; still with a body, but in the Spirit – no longer in the flesh. The last Adam became a life-giving spirit: And so it is written, *"The first man Adam became a living being. The last Adam became a life-giving spirit."* (I Corinthians 15:45 NKJV) In respect of His divinity the Lord Jesus remains uniquely "the only begotten Son of God." However, there is a sense in which from the resurrection and throughout eternity, He is also the *first begotten*, and His life from that time is found in many brethren. For we who are born of the Spirit are made, "partakers of the divine nature" (see 2 Peter 1:4), and that not of ourselves, but only in dependence of God and by virtue of our being "in Christ."

We have received the Spirit of adoption, whereby we cry, Abba, Father. The Spirit Himself bears witness with our spirit, that we are the children of God (see Romans 8:15, 16). It was through the *Incarnation* and the Cross that the Lord Jesus made this possible. The Father-heart of God was satisfied, for in the Son's obedience unto death the Father has secured His many sons.

In the first and the twentieth chapters of John are so precious. Notice, in the beginning of his Gospel John tells us that Jesus was "the only One from the Father. At the end of his Gospel, he tells us how, after He had died and risen again, Jesus said to Mary Magdalene, "Go unto My brethren, and say to them, I ascend unto My Father and your Father, and My God and your God." (see John 20:17). Now, in the resurrection, He adds, " ... and your Father." It is the eldest Son, the first begotten speaking. By His death and resurrection many brethren have been brought into God's family, and so, in the same verse He uses this very name for them, "calling them "My brethren." Thus, He affirms that He is not ashamed to call them brethren (see Hebrew 2:11).

WE ARE ALL OF ONE

What we have today in Christ is more than Adam lost. Adam was only a developed man. He remained only a developed man and never possessed the life of God. But when we receive the Son of God, not only do we receive the forgiveness of sins; we also receive the *divine life* which was represented in the Garden by the *tree of life*. So, by the new birth we possess what Adam missed, for we receive a life he never had.

God's desire is for sons who shall be joint heirs with Christ in glory. That is His goal; but how can He bring that about? Let's look at Hebrews 2:10-11: *"For it was fitting for Him, for whom are all things, and through whom are all things, in bringing many sons unto glory, to perfect the originator of their salvation through sufferings. For both He who sanctifies and those who are sanctified are all of one Father for this reason He is not ashamed to call them brothers [and sisters]."* NASB

STUDY GUIDE: CHAPTER 3 YOUR FAITH MUST BE VISIBLE

1. Faith that works must _____, and it must be _____.

2. Salvation is a _____, " … eternal life from God.

3. In the parable of the Sower, Jesus addressed those who never show any _____ of their _____ _____.

4. The Holy Spirit brings _____ and _____, which stem from believing the gospel by faith.

5. Death is an _____ _____ of the life of God.

6. God put two trees in the Garden so that Adam might exercise _____ _____.

7. God's desire is for _____ who shall be joint heirs with Christ in glory.

CHAPTER FOUR

This Is That

"The love of God has been poured out within our hearts through the Holy Spirit who was given to us." (Romans 5:5 NASB)

"If anyone does not have the Spirit of Christ, he does not belong to Him." (Romans 8:9 NASB)

We have spoken of the eternal purpose of God as the motive and explanation for all His dealings with us. We must digress in order to consider something which lies in the heart of all our experience as the vitalizing power for effective life and service. I speak of the personal presence of the Holy Spirit of God.

God does not give His gifts at random, nor dispense with them in a reckless manner. They are given freely to all, but they are given for a specific purpose. God has truly "blessed us with every spiritual blessing in the heavenly places in Christ" (see Ephesians 1:3). However, if those blessings which are ours in Christ are to become ours *in experience,* we must know on what ground we can appropriate them.

As we consider the *gift* of the Holy Spirit it is helpful to think of this in two aspects, as the Spirit outpoured and the Spirit indwelling. Our purpose now is to understand on what basis this twofold *gift* of the Holy Spirit becomes ours.

THE SPIRIT POURED OUT

Once we see the value of this *gift* of the outpoured Holy Spirit, and realize our deep need of it, we should ask, how can I receive the Holy Spirit in this way, to equip me with spiritual gifts and to empower me for God's service? Upon what basis has the Holy Spirit been given to His children? Let us turn first to Acts 2:32-36:

> *This Jesus hath God raised up, whereof we all are witnesses. Therefore being by the right hand of God exalted and having received of the Father the promise of the Holy Ghost, he hath shed forth this, which ye now see and hear. For David is not ascended into the heavens: but he saith himself, the LORD said unto my Lord, Sit thou on my right hand, until I make thy foes thy footstool. Therefore let all the house of Israel know assuredly, that God hath made that made this same Jesus, whom ye have crucified, both Lord and Christ.*

Peter states that the Lord Jesus was *exalted* at the right hand of God; resulting in His receiving of the Father the promise of the Holy Ghost. The miracle of Pentecost followed! Thus, the result of His exaltation was – this which you see and hear. What basis then, was the Spirit poured out on His people. Jesus was *exalted.*

- Because the Lord Jesus died on the Cross, I have received forgiveness of sins.
- Because the Lord Jesus rose from the grave, I received new life.
- Because the Lord Jesus has been exalted to the right hand of the Father, I have received the outpoured Spirit.

All is because of Him – nothing is because of me.

- Remission of sins is not based on human merit – but on the Lord's crucifixion.
- Regeneration is not based on human merit – but on the Lord's resurrection.
- The enduement of the Holy Spirit is not based on human merit – but on the Lord's exaltation.

The Holy Spirit has not been poured out on you or me to prove how great we are – but to prove the greatness of the Son of God. The principle on which we receive the enduement of the Holy Spirit is the same as that on which we receive the forgiveness of sins. Jesus has been *crucified*; therefore our sins have been forgiven – Jesus has been *glorified*; therefore the Spirit has been poured out upon us. Is it possible that the Son of God shed His Blood and your sins have not been forgiven? No! Then is it possible that the Son of God has been *glorified* and you have not received the Spirit? No!

If we lack the *experience,* we must ask God for revelation knowledge of this eternal truth, that the baptism of the Holy Spirit is the gift of the exalted Lord to His Church. Once we understand that, all effort will cease, and our prayer will give place to praise! It was *revelation* knowledge of what the Lord had done for the whole world that caused us to end *our own efforts* to secure forgiveness of sins, and it is a *revelation* of what the Lord has done for His Church that will bring us to an end of *our own efforts* to secure the baptism of the Holy Spirit. We work because we have not seen the work of Christ. However, once we have received that, *faith* will spring up in our hearts – as we believe, *experience* follows. As with forgiveness, so equally with the coming upon us of the Holy Spirit, again, all is a question of *faith!* The Spirit has been poured out to prove Christ's goodness and greatness, not ours. Christ has been crucified; therefore, we have been forgiven; Christ has been glorified; therefore we have been endued with power from on high - it is all because of Him!

THE SPIRIT INDWELLING

The Holy Spirit is the Spirit of truth. In John 14:16, Jesus promised that the Father would give the gospel believer another [*same kind as Himself*] Helper that He may abide with you forever. The Spirit would come indwell and help you forever (study Romans 8:9; 1 Corinthians 6:19-20; 12:13). When He, the Spirit of truth has come, *He will guide you into all truth … He will tell you things to come … He will glorify Me … He will take of Mine and declare it unto you.* The purpose of the Holy Spirit's coming is not condemnation, but conviction of the need for the Savior (see v. 13).

The Holy Spirit's *indwelling* of gospel believers as the source of truth, faith, and life is throughout redemptive history. Satan uses traditional and cultural Christianity to hinder and keep true believers from being able to demonstrate the power and display the gospel of grace as Christ commanded; that way he limits the impact of what a truly transformed life should have on the world. Today many churches have no demonstration of supernatural power. Such churches have a form of godliness [works-based salvation] but deny the supernatural power [the Holy Spirit]. This is not God's will for His church. Notice in John 14:15-31, Jesus promises His church supernatural blessings the kingdom of this world does not enjoy:

A supernatural Helper (vv. 15-16)
A supernatural life (vv. 18-19)
A supernatural union (vv. 20-25)
A supernatural Teacher (v. 26)
A supernatural peace (vv. 27.31)

These supernatural blessings are for all believers. They are embedded in our love for Jesus Christ as evidenced by our love for Him and others as we stand in obedience by our love for Him and others as we stand in obedience to His commands. Love and obedience are inseparable and are manifested in us by *fruit* produced by God in the transforming, regenerating power of the Holy Spirit. God has implanted within our hearts overflowing evidence that we belong to Him in that we love the One who first loved us (see Romans 5:5).

Once we see the value of this gift of God and come to the realization of our own deep need of it, we should immediately ask, "How can I receive the Holy Spirit in this way – to *equip me* with spiritual gifts[4] and *empower me* for God's service?"

---

[4]   A Definition – "Spirit gifts" (Gk. *Charisma*, "grace gifts") are various measures of divine grace, or power, by which the Lord Jesus through the Holy Spirit enables His people to perform special ministries in His work of building the Church (see 1 Corinthians 12:1-11; Romans 12:3, 6; 1 Peter 4:11).

THIS IS THAT

When our eyes are opened to see that the Spirit has already been poured out because Jesus has already been *glorified,* then prayer turns to praise in our hearts. All spiritual blessings come to us on a specific basis. God's gifts are freely given, but there are conditions of receiving the outpoured Spirit: Then Peter said unto them,

> *"Repent and be baptized every one of you in the name of Jesus Christ for the remission of sins, and ye shall receive the gift of the Holy Spirit. For the promise is unto you, and to your children, and to all that are afar off, even as many as the Lord our God shall call."* (Acts 2:38, 39 KJV)

Notice, four things are mentioned in this passage:

1. Repentance – means a changed mind. In times gone by, I thought sin was an enjoyable past time (now I've changed My mind). I thought the world was very attractive (now I know Better). I thought being a Christian was a miserable life (now I think differently). Once I thought certain things in the world were great (now I know different). There are some things I thought were utterly worthless (now I think they are most precious). I had a change of mind, I repented!

2. Baptism – is an outward expression of an inward faith. When in my heart I genuinely believe that I have died, have been buried, and have risen with Christ, then I should seek to be baptized (faith in action).

   Repentance and baptism are two divinely appointed conditions of forgiveness – *repentance and faith* publicly expressed. Have you openly testified publicly of your union with Christ?

3. Forgiveness – Because Jesus died on the cross, I have received forgiveness of my sins; because the Lord Jesus rose from the dead,

I have in Him received new life. Without shedding of blood there is no remission (see Hebrews 9:22).

4. The Holy Spirit – Because the Lord Jesus has been *exalted to the right hand of the father,* I have received the outpoured Spirit.

The Holy Spirit has not been poured out on you or me because of any greatness in us, but to prove the greatness of Jesus Christ, the Son of God (see v. 33).

The purpose of Pentecost is to prove the Lordship of Jesus Christ. Verses 37-41 describe the immediate results of Pentecost; Peter explains the unusual events in terms of the outpouring of the Spirit predicted by Joel's messianic words. The outpouring of the Spirit in the Old Testament had been largely reserved for the spiritual and national leaders of Israel. Under the New Covenant, however, the authority of the Spirit is for "all flesh," all who are under the New Covenant. Every believer is anointed to be a priest and king to God.

THE POWER OF THE CROSS

There is substantial evidence showing that the supernatural miracles, and healing ministry and supernatural spiritual gifts are the chief demonstrations of the redeeming power of the cross that accompanied the preaching of the gospel in the New Testament church. The cross is the heart of the gospel, the gravity of the New Testament *faith.* We must preach the cross and all the power in and through it. That includes the atonement, repentance, forgiveness of sins and the manifestation of miraculous deeds.

The cross is the foundation for all God's works in our world today. It is the base to forgive, restore lives, heal brokenness in people and touch our physical needs. Signs and wonders reveal the nature of God. The Scripture speaks clearly about the Holy Spirit's prevalence in our world. I pray we will believe in the full range of the Holy Spirit's activity throughout the church age as a vital part of preaching the gospel, including miracles, healings, signs and wonders. Let us believe, teach and admonish, equip and release people to unlock the supernatural power of the Holy Spirit. Sadly, we know that the church has suffered from a twisted theology concerning miracles, healings and the supernatural.

Many theologians, teachers, and preachers have taught that the age of miracles ceased with the apostolic period of the church and that God no longer heals people as He did in the first century. Perhaps that's why so many deny the greatest miracle:

In cooperation with the Father (see Galatians1:1) and the Son (see John 10:18), the Holy Spirit participated in bringing about Jesus' physical resurrection from the dead (see Romans 8:1; Ephesians 1:19-20). He provided the new life force that made Jesus' dead body *alive* and that will change the bodies of His people to a *"spiritual body"* (see 1 Corinthians 15:44). He also changed Jesus' body, which had been created to live on the earth, so that it could exist forever in the eternal state (see 1 Corinthians 15:45).

THE DESTINATION OF SAVED PEOPLE

1. Before Jesus' resurrection, all saved people who died were taken to a place of bliss in hades (OT sheol; Psalms16:10, KJV hell). This was also known as "paradise," or "Abraham's Bosom" (see Luke 16:19-31; 23:43).
2. Since the Lord Jesus' resurrection, paradise has been removed to heaven (see 2 Corinthians 12:2, 4). At death all gospel believers are immediately taken to heaven to be with the Lord Jesus (study carefully 2 Corinthians 5:6, 8; Philippians 1:21-26; Revelation 14:1-5).

THE DESTINATION OF UNSAVED PEOPLE

In the future, the divine judicial punishment for sin that unsaved people will experience will be everlasting spiritual death, or "the second death" (see Revelation 20:14). This everlasting death is the *event* of their being cast into hell, or the lake of fire (v. 15). By this event they will enter the *everlasting state* of unrelieved suffering and absolute isolation from God (Matthew 25:46; 2 Thessalonian 1:9; (see Revelation 14:10-11). Upon death unsaved people are taken to hades (OT sheol) and are confined there until the resurrection of their bodies and their judgment (see Luke 16:23; John 5:28-29; Revelation 20:13). After their resurrection and judgment, the unsaved are cast into the lake of fire (Revelation 20:11-15).

JUDGMENT BEFORE THE GREAT WHITE THRONE

Then I saw a great white throne and Him who was seated on it. From His presence earth and sky fled away, and no place was found for them. And I saw the dead, great and small standing before the throne, and the books were opened. Then another book was opened, which was the book of life. And the dead were judged by what was written in the books, according to what they had done. And the sea gave up the dead who were in it, Death and Hades gave up their dead who were in them, and they were judged, each one according to what they had done. Then death and hades were throne thrown into the lake of fire. This is the second death, the lake of fire. And if anyone's name was not found written in the book of life, he [or she] was put into the lake of fire. (Revelation 20:11-15 ESV) Emphasis added.

Jay Leach

STUDY GUIDE: CHAPTER FOUR THIS IS THAT

1. The gift of the Holy Spirit is helpful in two aspects, as the Spirit _____ _____ and the Spirit _____.

2. The Lord Jesus was _____ at the right -hand of God.

3. The enduement of the Holy Spirit is not based on _____ _____ but on the Lord's exaltation.

4. If we lack the _____ we must ask God for revelation knowledge of eternal truth.

5. The Holy Spirit's indwelling of gospel believers as the _____ of truth, faith, and life throughout redemptive _____.

6. The Holy Spirit _____ in bringing about Jesus' physical _____.

7. At death all gospel believers are _____ _____ _____ to be with the Lord Jesus (see 2 Cor. 5:6, 8).

SECTION TWO

THE
SPIRIT-WORD
IN TANDEM

CHAPTER FIVE

Don't Divorce The Holy Spirit

Even the Spirit of truth; whom the world cannot
receive, because it seeth him not,
neither knoweth him: but you know him,
for he dwelleth with you and shall be in you.
John 14:17 KJV

As with forgiveness, so equally with the coming upon us of the Holy Spirit. The whole question is one of faith. We walk by faith not by sight. The Spirit has been poured out upon us – because Jesus is on the throne (see Ephesians 1:19-22). There, the Lord Jesus continues His Messianic work as our great High Priest (see Hebrews 4:14-16) and waits until the Father makes His enemies His footstool at His second coming to earth (see 1:12-13; Revelation 19:15).

Christ has been crucified; therefore we have been forgiven. Christ has been glorified; therefore, we have been endued with power from on high. It is all because of Him! Praise God!

GRACE AND THE HOLY SPIRIT

Divine grace portrays God in action, doing for us that we cannot do for ourselves. In fact, we need to get our "self" totally out of the way so that the Holy Spirit can direct and guide us. With the help of this grace (unmerited favor/power), generated by the activity of the Holy Spirit – we can be the kind of people He wants us to be and do the things He wants us to do (see 1 Corinthians 15:10; 2 Corinthians 1:12). Also by God's grace/power we make the best of our circumstances (2 Corinthians 12:8-10).

Implementing this grace, the Holy Spirit stands ready to *enable* us to do and to be all that God requires of our lives, like:

1. Expressing Christian character (see Galatians 5:22-23; Ephesians 5:9),
2. Doing God's will (see Philippians 2:13),
3. Waging victorious warfare against our spiritual enemies (see Galatians 5:16),
4. Performing Christian service (Acts 1:8; 1 Corinthians 15:10), and
5. Rendering to God acceptable worship (see Philippians 3:3; John 4:24).

In fact, we can do these things only by the vitality of Jesus' spiritual life, which is conveyed to us by the Holy Spirit (see Philippians 4:13; Hebrews 13:21; John 15:3).

To receive help from the Holy Spirit, we must be filled with the Spirit, which allows Him to work in our lives:

> *Wherefore be ye not unwise but understanding what the will of the Lord is.' And be not drunk with wine, wherein is excess; but be filled with the Spirit; Speaking to yourselves in psalms and hymns and spiritual songs, singing and making melody in your heart to the Lord;' Giving thanks always for all things unto God and the Father in the name of our Lord Jesus Christ; Submitting yourselves to one another in the fear of God.* (see Ephesians 5:17-21 KJV).

Our continuous (being filled with the Spirit) v. 18, surrendering to His control does not make us passive instruments in His hand. We must still exhibit the right attitudes, fulfill our commitments, and perform our duties. But we must do (all) these things in union with the Holy Spirit by looking to Him to *direct* and *to help us/empower* to do them in a manner that will glorify God.

WHAT WE MISS – "IF"

All of these many supernatural blessings are for all gospel believers. They are embedded in our love for Jesus Christ as evidenced by our love for Him and others as we stand in obedience to His commands.

This love is manifested though His glorious Presence in each true believer. Sandwiched between chapters 12 and 14 of I Corinthians is chapter 13 called the love chapter; where we are told, *"the greatest of these is love."* Chapter 12 lists the gifts of the Spirit and chapter 14 records the operation of the gifts; however as mentioned earlier, to get from chapter 12 and the gifts listings, to operate in the body of Christ (chapter 14 requires all believers to go through chapter 13 – love! The gifts of the Spirit can operate properly only through the love of God shed abroad in our hearts in the new birth, our God-like love (see Romans 5:5).

STUDY GUIDE: CHAPTER FIVE DON'T' DIVORCE THE HOLY SPIRIT

1. We walk by _____ not by _____.

2. _____ _____ portrays God in action.

3. Christ has been crucified; therefore we have been _____.

4. We must look to the Holy Spirit to direct and to _____ us.

5. This love is _____ through His glorious Presence in each _____ _____.

6. These many supernatural _____ are for all gospel _____.

7. 1 Corinthians 13 is called the _____ _____.

CHAPTER SIX

Spirit And Word

For we are God's fellow workers, you are God's field,
you are God's building. According to the grace of God,
which was given to me, as a wise master builder I have
laid the foundation, and another builds on it. For no other
foundation can anyone lay than that which is laid, which is
Jesus Christ. (I Corinthians 3:9-11 NKJV)

The foundation we are building on is Christ, and our blueprint is the Bible. The most effective way of accomplishing anything is using a game plan. Coaches do it, military commanders do, and so should we. An architect does not build any project without a blueprint being drawn first.

The pressing need today is for church leaders to think innovatively, at the same time keeping the church on its Gospel mission – churches that are biblically based and that spiritually transform people into fruitful disciples of Christ. This is not a small task in today's complex church world. It seems that leadership preparation has not equipped leaders to face today's cultural and theological challenges, organizational changes, and tremendous pressures to succeed.

Church leaders today are expected to provide effective leadership in the middle of a changing context that faces a major and massive cultural shift in people's attitude toward God, Christ, the Holy Spirit, the Bible, the church, and church leadership. Inadequately trained leaders are vulnerable to the many strong voices teaching various church models to follow and various success stories, all of which influence the leaders' thinking and actions. Today leaders seemingly face insurmountable obstacles to building churches for which they have a *God-vision*. Many lose heart and a clear vision for the church, and become unfocused, double-minded and, consequently, not have faith to make future plans and hard changes.

CHRIST LOVED THE CHURCH

Christ loved the church so much that He gave His life for her. In His three-and-a-half-year long ministry on earth. He interacted with all kinds of people getting into their world – healed them, delivered them and ultimately died for them. His church is a place of freedom from sin and oppression, of faith and victory. It is a community of God's people thinking and acting as God intended and inviting others to join the family. Today, we have the authority and responsibility to help Him build His church of which He is the foundation (study Matthew 16:18-19; also 1 Peter 2:4-6).

When Jesus left this earth, He gave His disciples all the tools needed to construct His church. Fitted with a toolbox full of the Holy Spirit's and Christ's teachings, the apostles did build lives and a viable church – as we see in the book of Acts. It is their ... example and teachings, along with Christ's that we follow when we conceptualize and plan our churches today. Again, the foundation we are building on is Christ, and our blueprint is the Word of God in tandem with the Holy Spirit.

BLENDING THE SPIRIT AND THE WORD

My hunger in knowing and understanding the Word of God have led me to a path of knowledge, including Bible colleges and universities. I also took classes at other schools, both Baptist and those with Pentecostal/ Charismatic orientations. The Baptist would say that the Pentecostals have little or no scriptural foundation and that they are shallow and driven by personalities and unscriptural manifestations. The Pentecostals would counter that the Baptist have no spiritual power, being spiritually shallow and dry as Ezekiel's boneyard, driven by knowledge not power. Some chided with name calling, for example the "frozen chosen." My wife and I are a blend of both being raised Baptist, caught up in the charismatic movement (in the 60's) and filled with the Holy Spirit.

My Baptist beginning instilled the value and conviction of sound doctrine. The Charismatic movement and my encounter with the Holy Spirit ignited a passion for discipleship, preaching and teaching the Word, and seeing miracles, healings and powerful works of the Holy Spirit. Our journey has kept us loving both the Spirit and the Word. Through the years as I study the church in Scripture, I am convinced that an effective, God-pleasing church is not exclusively Spirit driven or exclusively Bible exposition driven – but a precise blend of both. It is a church built on solid biblical knowledge, proper interpretation and respect for doctrinal truth – and energized and anointed by the Spirit so that the *gifts of the Spirit* flows through every person. A determined balance of the Spirit and the Word should characterize our preaching, teaching, and corporate services. The Spirit-Word balance is a defining characteristic of a New Testament Church.

From Creation the Spirit and the Word have worked together, as seen in Genesis 1:2-3: "The earth was without form, and void, darkness covered the face of the deep and the Spirit of God was hovering over the waters. Then God said, "Let there be light" and there was light." The Spirit of God hovered over the deep, preparing the way for the coming of the Word.

THE UNIVERSE WAS CREATED WITH A WORD – AND GIVEN LIFE THROUGH THE HOLY SPIRIT.

There followed a universe created with a word (God's Word) and given life through the Holy Spirit. Likewise, The New Testament Church is a place where a group of believers who have accepted Christ (the Word) are bonded together by new birth through the Holy Spirit and are endued with His power to effectively carry out the work of God. Our lives and churches must have both – it's biblical!

THE SPIRIT-WORD CHURCH IN ACTS

The Spirit-Word balance is seen throughout Scripture particularly in the Book of Acts, as the norm for church life.

THE SPIRIT CHURCH

Acts 1:8 – "But you shall receive power when the *Holy Spirit* has come upon you; and you shall be witnesses to Me in Jerusalem, and in all Judea and Samaria, and to the end of the earth."

Acts 2:4 – "And they were all filled with the *Holy Spirit* and began to speak with other tongues, as the Spirit gave them utterance."

Acts 2:33 – "Therefore being exalted to the right hand of God and having received from the Father the promise of the *Holy Spirit,* He poured out this which you now see and hear."

"Then the churches throughout a Judea, Galilee and Samaria had peace and were edified. And walking in the fear of the Lord and in the comfort of the *Holy Spirit,* they were multiplied." See also: Acts 4:8; Acts 4:31; Acts 6:3; Acts 8:17; Acts 9:31; Acts 10: 44.

THE WORD CHURCH

Acts 2:41 – "Then those who gladly received the *word* were baptized; and that day about three thousand souls were added to them."

Acts 4:4 – "However, many of those who heard the *word* believed, and the number of men came to be about five thousand."

Acts 4:29 – "Now, Lord, look on their threats, and grant to Your servant that with all boldness they may speak Your *word*."

Acts 6:7 – "Then the *word* of God spread, and the number of the disciples multiplied greatly in Jerusalem, and a great many of the priests were obedient to the truth."

Acts 8:4 – "Therefore those who were scattered went everywhere preaching the *word*."

Acts 15:35-36 – "Paul and Barnabas also remained in Antioch, teaching and preaching the *word* of the Lord, with many others also. Then after some days Paul and Barnabas, "Let us now go back and visit our brethren in every city where we have preached the *word* of the Lord and see how they are doing."

Acts 19:20 – "So the *word* of the Lord grew mightily and prevailed."

See also Acts 13:5; 15:35-36; 16:17; 17:11, 13; 18:11; 19:10; 28

CHURCH LEADERSHIP

The leadership team of the church must highly regard both the Spirit and the Word as equal strengths for building every aspect of the church (see Matthew 16:16-18; Acts 2:1-4). These leaders will model both aspects in their life living and ministry. They will exhibit spirit leadership by living in the Holy Spirit and being full of the Spirit (see Judges 6:34; 2 Kings 2:9; 1 Timothy 4:2).

In the beginning of Acts 2, the birth of the church exploded with the *outpouring* of the Holy Spirit. From this founding experience, we can gain invaluable standards, and characteristics of a church that is born by the Holy Spirit and is formed and empowered by Him. Additionally, the Spirit used wind and fire to manifest His presence and establish the church. When we believe God is truly present in our churches by His amazing presence and power, the church is ready to be the church.

As a leadership team, we must continually evaluate and make necessary adjustments to keep the healthy blending of the Spirit and the Word (see 1 Thess. 5:19-21; Titus 1:9).

A COMMITMENT TO BLEND

In his book, *Strategic Church,* Frank Damazio says, "A strategic leader builds a church that is *committed* to interfusing and intermixing the Spirit and the Word in parts." The Spirit and the Word are equal. To hold both together Church history proves an intensely difficult and elusive challenge; that we cannot afford to fail to meet. This is a commitment to blend:

- Holy Spirit *activity* and Word of God *basics,*
- Holy Spirit *ministry* and Word of God *principles,*
- Holy Spirit *speaking* and Word of God *guidelines,*
- Holy Spirit *worship* and Word of God *substance,*
- Holy Spirit *power* and Word of God *parameters,*
- Holy Spirit *presence* and Word of God *approach,*
- Holy Spirit *guidance* and Word of God *disciplines,*
- Holy Spirit *creativity* and Word of God *authority,*
- Holy Spirit-*inspired vision* and Word of God *definition of the vision,* and
- Holy Spirit *revelation* and Word of God *interpretation.*[5]

I believe most successful church builders agree that the Spirit-Word foundation not only provides a solid base, but also a clear path to follow with faith. A dedicated commitment to following consistently biblical, time-tested, principles over an extended period leads to authentic worthy results of long-lasted spiritual fruit.

---

[5] Frank Damazio, *Strategic Church* published by (Baker Books Publishing 2014) 198

STUDY GUIDE: CHAPTER SIX SPIRIT AND WORD

1. Christ loved the church so much that He _____ His life
    _____ _____.

2. Christ's church is a place of _____ from _____ and
    _____ of faith and victory.

3. The foundation we are building on today is _____.

4. From Creation the _____ and the _____ have worked
    together as seen in Genesis 1:2-3.

5. A determined balance of the Spirit and the Word should characterize
    our _____, _____, and corporate services.

6. In the beginning of Acts 2 the birth of the church exploded with the
    outpouring of the Holy Spirit.

7. We can gain invaluable _____ and _____ of a
    church that is born by the Holy Spirit and empowered by Him.

CHAPTER SEVEN

Don't Be Fooled

The fool has said in his heart,
"There is no God."
They are corrupt.
They have done abominable works,
There is none who does good.
The Lord looks down from heaven
upon the children of men,
To see if there are any who
understand, who seek God.
They have all turned aside,
They have together become corrupt.
There is none who does good,
No, not one. (Psalm 14:1-3 NKJV)

This Psalm, which is closely similar to Psalm 53 is a wisdom psalm attributed to David. It speaks of the *foolishness* of living as if God does not exist. The Psalm has three movements. The word fool here does not refer to mental instability. The phrase "no God" which seems to be the thought of most people in this country today suggests "practical atheism."

Growing in popularity today, many who claim to be Christians fit in this category. This view says, even if God does exist it has no bearing on one's life. This is the viewpoint of Psalms 10:4:

> *The wicked in his proud*
> *countenance does not seek God*
> *God is in none of his thoughts.*

God is *not* in his thoughts is the most difficult part of his circumstances. People went about then just as increasing numbers are doing today. This person has no thought of God; and his or her wicked enemies are able to boast in themselves. Many turn reality upside down by boasting themselves, by praising evil and shunning God. In Ps. 14:2-3 the psalmist reports, the Lord looks down where His inquiry leads to judgment as in (see Genesis 6:12). The fact is the Lord is omniscience of God, which means He knows everything. He knows our frame. No not one. The biblical teaching on depravity[6] is not that each individual is as evil as he or she could possibly be, but that sin is present in every individual (study (carefully Romans 3). Since no one is perfect, all must ask God for forgiveness – something He freely gives to those who place their faith in His Son. As we stated in an earlier section, that is why we were crucified with Christ to die in Him and be resurrected in Him. We are a new creation!

All that we were of Adam had to go. (see 2 Corinthians 5:17) and prayerfully study Romans 5). "In Him we have redemption through His blood, the forgiveness of sins, according to the riches of His grace which He made to abound toward us in wisdom and prudence, having made known to us the mystery of His will, according to His good pleasure which He purposed in Himself, that in this dispensation of the fullness of the times He might gather in one all things in Christ both which are in heaven, and which are on earth – in Him."(Ephesians 17:7-19 NKJV)

"If we say that we have no sin, we deceive ourselves, and the truth is not in us. If we confess our sins, He is faithful and just to forgive us our sins and to cleanse us from all unrighteousness." (1 John 1:8-9 NKJV)

---

[6] The Oxford dictionary defines depravity as the state of corruption of human nature due to original sin. This does not mean every person is as sinful as they could possibly be, but it does mean though that every part of a person has been corrupted.

PRACTICAL FAITH

Practical faith is that 24/7 trust in God and His Word that we who are saved are to exercise during the course of our daily living (see Galatians 2:20; 2 Corinthians5:7).

I have been crucified with Christ; and it is no longer I who live, but Christ lives in me; and the life which I now live in the flesh I live by faith in the Son of God, who loved me and gave Himself up for me. (Galatians 2:20 NASB)

"For we walk by faith, not by sight." (2 Corinthians 5:7 NASB)

"For I am not ashamed of the Gospel of Christ, for it is the power of God for salvation to *everyone who believes...*" (see Romans 1:16 NASB). In the letter to the Romans we find Paul's clearest and most detailed explanation of the gospel message. He explains that the Good News of Christ is the power of God for salvation for everyone who believes. The Greek word for *salvation* used by Paul literally means *"deliverance" or "preservation."* In a spiritual context, the idea to is rescue from the power and dominion of sin.

A LIVING SACRIFICE

Paul portrays Jesus Christ on the basis of His sacrificial death on the Cross in the place of sinners, as the Author and Provider of salvation (see Romans 3:24, 25; 5;21; Acts 4:12; Hebrews 12:2). Those who repent and trust in Jesus will experience its blessings (see John 3:16; Ephesians 2:8, 9; Hebrews 2:3). The blessings Paul is talking about are justification, sanctification, and glorification:

Justification – is the judicial act wherein God, acquits and declares the gospel believer to be righteous *for He made Him so.* We who are saved were saved on account of their faith in Jesus. He paid for their sins completely and finally on the Cross, and through faith in Him their sins can be forgiven (see Romans 3:21; 4:5; 5:1). Closely related to justification is regeneration, in which the Spirit of God indwells a repentant sinner and imparts eternal life to his or her spiritually dead spirit (see Ephesians 2:1-5).

The need of *unsaved people for justification* is seen in their condemnation by God and their lack of acceptable righteousness (see

John 3:18). To be condemned is to be found guilty of a crime and sentenced to punishment. God has already found *unsaved people* guilty of original sin (see Romans 3:23). In their rebellion against Him, they substitute their own ethical standards of conduct for what He requires of them. But this *self-righteousness* is not acceptable to Him (see Isaiah 64:6). God declares that no one is righteous in His sight without His gift of righteousness through faith in His Son (see Romans 3:10, 22; 1 Corinthians 1:30).

We who are saved were *graciously* justified *by Jesus' blood,* that is by His atoning work (see Titus 3:7; Romans 5:9). In our *unsaved state,* we could neither deliver ourselves from divine condemnation nor attain the righteousness that God required of us. But in His *gracious love* (John 3:16; Titus 3:4). God provided the way whereby He could be just or righteous and still justify undeserving sinners (Romans 3:24-26). By His atoning work, the Lord Jesus dealt with our sins and paid their awful price (5:8; Hebrews 9:26).

Upon our faith in Jesus and His atoning work, God applied to our account the value of this sacrifice, acquitted us of condemnation, made us righteous in Jesus, and declared us to be righteous in His sight (Romans 5:16-17).

While Jesus' death atoned for our sins, the Lord's *resurrection* made this work effective for our justification (4:25). Like all other aspects of salvation, justification is a gracious divine work:

Being justified as a gift by His grace through the redemption which is in Christ Jesus (Romans 3:24).

So that being justified by His grace we would be made heirs according to the hope of eternal life (Titus 3:7).

Sanctification – is the process in which God develops the new life[7] of the gospel believer and gradually through the working of the indwelling

---

[7]   Unlike mysticism, which seeks contact with God by immediate intuition apart from His Word, Christian experience conforms to and is understood by the Bible's teachings about the subject.

Holy Spirit, and the Word, brings them to perfection (maturity). (see Romans 6:11; Philippians 1:6). We must keep in mind that, while the gospel believers have spiritual life by the new birth, they do not always express this new life in their daily behavior. Spirit-Word **disciplining** is needed to learn how to express this new life in our behavior to the glory of God. Like all growth, spiritual growth consists of the joint activity Spirit-Word and the saved person.

This is important. The growth experience of spiritual behavior is absolute, for we are either doing and being or not doing and being what God desires. Implementing this grace to help us, the Holy Spirit stands ready to enable us to do and to be all that God requires of our lives, like:

- Expressing Christian character (see Galatians 5:22-23; Ephesians 5:9)
- Doing God's will (see Philippians 2:13)
- Waging victorious warfare against our spiritual enemies (see Galatians 5:16)
- Performing Christian service (see Acts 1:8; 1 Corinthians 15:10)
- Rendering God acceptable worship (see Philippians 3:3; John 4:24)

In fact, we can do these things only by the vitality of Jesus' spiritual life, which is conveyed to us by the Holy Spirit (see Philippians 4:13; Hebrews 13:21; John 15:5).

To obtain the Holy Spirit's help, we must receive His filling, which allows Him to work in our lives (see Ephesians 5:18). Our surrender to His control does not make us passive instruments in His hand. But we must do these things in union with the Holy Spirit by looking to Him to direct and help us do them in a way that will glorify God.

Glorification – is the ultimate salvation of the whole person. This occurs when we are face to face with our Savior in His coming kingdom. At that time, God will completely mold us into the image of Christ:

> *For those whom He foreknew, He also predestined to become conformed to the image of His Son, so that He would be the first-born among many brothers and sisters* (Romans 8:29 NASB).

Who will transform the body of our lowly condition into conformity with His glorious body, by the exertion of the power that He has even to subject all things to Himself (Philippians 3:21 NASB). Then we will be able to enjoy complete fellowship with God forever.

NONE BUT THE RIGHTEOUS

"For in it (the gospel) the righteousness of God is revealed from faith to faith;[8] as it is written, *"But the righteous one will live by faith."* (Romans 1:17 NASB). Although Satan has been defeated by the Lord Jesus in every contest thus far, he is still very active in his warfare against his former earthly subjects, the Lord's people (see Colossians 1:13). However, we who are saved (the righteous) can have opportunities of victory over this adversary as we prepare for the conflict and take Scriptural steps that lead us to victory.

I say, "opportunities of victory," but if we fail to do our part, we shall be briefly defeated by the adversary. God can only give us victory in our battles with the devil as we look to Him to help us (see James 4:7). These defeats do not determine the outcome of the campaign, although they affect our testimony and hinder our spiritual progress.

One day when Jesus completes His Church, the Lord will remove His righteous people from the scene of this spiritual warfare (carefully study Galatians 1:4; 1 Thessalonians 4:13-18). To win a victory over the enemy, we must prepare for his attacks and take steps that lead to victory when he attacks. Also, we must always be on the alert for his next move.

PREPARATION FOR BATTLE

By now we should have discovered that natural weapons including talking ability, money, politics, education, power and influence will not help us in our fight with these unseen spiritual enemies. Paul wants us to know whom our battle is against.

He says,

---

[8] From faith to faith means faith is at the beginning of the salvation process, and it is the goal as well. When a person first exercises faith in Christ, that person is saved from the penalty of sin and declared righteous. As the believer lives by faith, God continues to save him or her from the power of sin to live righteously.

"For we wrestle not against flesh and blood, but against principalities, against powers, against the rulers of the darkness of the world, against spiritual wickedness in high places" (Ephesians 6:12).

Notice the real adversaries are unseen hosts of wicked spirits working behind the scenes through the devil's children and fleshly Christians. However, he can do nothing with the gospel believer unless we allow the flesh to cooperate with them. These demonic forces come to tempt, seduce, deceive, and assault our flesh and minds. That's why the flesh must be dealt with before we attempt to deal with the devil and his hosts.

By living a sustained crucified and sanctified life, we are able to neutralize any attack the enemy tries to war against our flesh. How is this true? Dead people don't have the capacity to respond to temptation, and deception. So, the majority of these demonic attacks against us will never succeed if we are living the sustained crucified life and reckoning ourselves to be "dead to sin" daily:

"Knowing this, that our old man was crucified with Him, that the body of sin might be done away with, that we should no longer be slaves to sin. For he who has died has been freed from sin. 'Likewise, you also, reckon yourselves to be dead indeed to sin, but alive to God in Christ Jesua our Lord" (Romans 6:6, 7, 11).

Some writers claim that the "old man" refers to a part of us, specifically our old Adamic nature and our sinful disposition. However, the word "man" does not refer only to a part of an individual; instead, it pertains to the entire inner person before conversion, because the person is connected to the sin nature of Adam. However, it is important that we "know" that not only the old man, but all that was in Adam was crucified with Christ (see Galatians 2:20).

Simply put, a gospel believer is not the same person he or she was before conversion; but now is a new creation in Christ (see 2 Corinthians 5:17). Those demonic allegations will have no power or control in your life (see Galatians 5:16-17).

Again, there are two reasons for crucifying the old man:

1. That the body of sin might be done away with.
2. That we should no longer be slaves to sin.

THE SPIRIT OF TRUTH

The Holy Spirit is the Spirit of Truth. In John 14:16, Jesus promised that the Father would give the true believer another *[same kind as Himself]* Helper *["one called alongside to help"]* that He may abide *[has to do with permanent residence in the believer]* be with you forever.

A gospel believer is not the same person he or she was before conversion; but now is a new creation in Christ (see 2 Corinthians 5:17).

The Spirit of Truth would come, indwell and helps the believer forever (see Romans 8:9; 1 Corinthians 6:19, 20; 12:12). The Holy Spirit's coming seems to have a dual purpose:

1. And when He is come, He will convict the world of sin – because they did not believe in Jesus as Messiah and the Son of God [rejecting the finished work of Christ] (see John 16:8).
2. When He the Spirit of Truth has come, He will guide you into all truth … He will tell you things to come … He will take of mine and declare it unto you.

The purpose of the Holy Spirit coming is not condemnation, but to [convince] the world of their need for the Savior (see v.13).

THE HOLY SPIRIT LAYS OUT JESUS' PLAN FOR HIS DISCIPLES

- Love is to serve as the distinguishing characteristic of discipleship (see John 13:35). This love is produced through the New Covenant by the transforming power of the Holy Spirit (see Jeremiah 31:29-34; Ezekiel 36:24-26; Galatians 5:22).

- He is the Spirit of Truth in that He is the source of truth, and he communicates the truth to His own by indwelling and teaching them to witness and proclaim the gospel (see v. 26; 16:12).
- Apart from Him, humankind cannot know God's truth (see 1 Corinthians 2:12-16; 1 John 2:20, 27).
- True gospel believers obey the Lord's commands by submitting to His Spirit and His Word.

The Holy Spirit's indwelling of believers indicates a distinction between the Holy Spirit's ministry before and after Pentecost. Clearly the Holy Spirit has been with all who ever believed throughout redemptive history as the source of truth, faith, and life. Jesus is saying something new is coming into His ministry. John 7:37-39 indicates this unique ministry will be like, "rivers of living water."

Please note the difference once more the Old Covenant believers that Paul encountered who had not received the Holy Spirit in the unique fullness and intimacy (see Acts 19:7; 1:8; 2:1-4; 1 Corinthians12:11-13). Satan uses philosophy, psychology and cultural Christianity to keep some true Christians from being able demonstrate the power and display the gospel of grace as Christ commanded; that way he can limit the impact a truly transformed life should have on the world.

Without the Holy Spirit's operation in local churches there can be no viable life, or demonstration of supernatural power. Such churches have a form of Godliness [works and cultural-based religion] which denies the power [the Holy Spirit]. This is not God's will for His church. In John 14:15-31, Jesus promises His church [body of Christ] supernatural blessings the kingdom of this world does not and cannot enjoy:

- A supernatural Helper (vv. 15-17).
- A supernatural life (vv. 18-19).
- A supernatural union (vv. 20-23).
- A supernatural Teacher (v. 26).
- A supernatural peace (vv. 27-31).

These supernatural blessings are for all gospel believers. They are embedded in our love for Jesus Christ as evidenced by our love for Him and others as we stand in obedience to His commands.

Love and obedience are inseparable and are manifested in us in *fruit* produced by God in the transforming, regenerating power of the Holy Spirit. God has placed within our hearts overflowing evidence that we belong to Him in that we love the One who first loved us (see Romans 5:5).

SUPERNATURAL LOVE

This love is manifested through His glorious Presence in each true believer. Sandwiched between chapters 12 and 14 of 1 Corinthians is chapter 13 called the love chapter; where we are told, "the greatest of these is love." In chapter 12 the gift listings are given; but how the gifts operate in the body of Christ requires you to go through chapter 13, love! The gifts of the Spirit can operate properly only through the love of God shed abroad in our hearts in the new birth, our God-like love.

Characteristics of that love

1. **It suffers long** – is patient (see 1 Thessalonians 5:14).
2. **It is kind** – gentle especially with those who hurt (see Ephesians 4:32).
3. **It does not envy** – is not jealous of what others have (see Proverbs 23:17).
4. **It does not parade itself** – put itself on display (see John 3:30).
5. **It is not puffed up** – arrogance, or pride (see Galatians 6:3).
6. **It does not act rudely** – mean-spiritedly, insulting others (see Ecclesiastes 5:2).
7. **It does not seek its own** – way or act pushy (1 Corinthians 10:24).
8. **It is not provoked** – or angered (see Proverbs 19:11).
9. **It thinks no evil** – does not keep score on others (see Hebrews 10:17).
10. **It rejoices not in iniquity** – takes no pleasure when others fall into sin (see Mark 3:5).

11. **It rejoices in the truth** – is joyful when righteousness prevails (see 2 John 4).
12. **It bears all things** – handles the burdensome (see Galatians 6:2).
13. **It believes all things** – trusts in God no matter what (Proverbs 3:5).
14. **It hopes all things** – keeps looking up, does not despair (see Philippians 3:13).
15. **It endures all things** – puts up with everything; does not wear out (see Galatians 6:9).
16. **It never fails** – the only thing it cannot do is fail (see 1 Corinthians 16:14).

The objects of faith and hope will be fulfilled and perfectly manifested in heaven, but love the God-like virtue, is everlasting (see 1 John 4:8). Heaven will be the place for the expression of anything but perfect love toward God and each other. The implication is that such children will be recognizable by God-like qualities.

THE SONS OF GOD

But as many as received Him, to them He gave the right to become children of God, to those who believe in His name, who were born, not of blood, nor of the will of the flesh, nor of the will of man, but of God. (John 1:12-13 NASB)

In Romans 8:14, the apostle Paul expounds on an identifiable trait of the children of God: *For all who are being led by the Spirit of God, these are the sons and daughters of God. NASB* Most believers do not have a clear understanding of what this involves. When most members of the local churches think of being led by the Spirit, they more than likely will picture in their minds a particular fellow Christian who makes reference to the fact that God told them to do something, and they felt compelled to obey.

Certainly hearing the voice of God and acting on it is part of what it means to be led of the Spirit of God. Being led of God's Spirit implies not only being obedient to the voice of God; but also the Holy Spirit is forming the character of Christ within us.

God's desire that the individual characters of His children undergo a transformational process and become identical with the character of Jesus, the apostle Paul plainly states,

> *For whom He did foreknow, He also did predestinate to be conformed to the image of His Son, that He might be the firstborn among many brethren.* (Romans 8:29)

Being conformed to the image of Jesus means taking on His form, His likeness, and His resemblance. When all of God's children are conformed to the character of Christ and the likeness of His only begotten Son, Jesus – then and only then will it become evident that they are led by the Spirit of God therefore truly they are the sons and daughters of God.

Developing the character of Christ is accomplished by developing the same fruit that were recognized in His life. In Matthew 7, Jesus Himself taught that it is through outward manifestation [fruit] that inward natural [character] is recognized. He warns beware of false prophets ... "you will know them by their fruit." (see Matthew 7:15, 16, 20).

STUDY GUIDE: CHAPTER SEVEN DON'T BE FOOLED

1. Psalm 14:1-3, speaks of the foolishness of living as if God
   _____ _____.

2. Psalm 10:4, speaks of the view which says, even if God does exist – it
   has no _____ on one life.

3. If we say that we have _____ _____ we _____
   ourselves and the truth is not in us.

4. The Greek word for salvation means
   _____ or _____.

5. Upon our faith in Jesus and His atoning work, God has declared us
   to be _____ in His sight.

6. The gospel believer is not the same person he or she was
   before _____.

7. Jesus warns, beware of false _____ ... you will know them
   by their _____.

CHAPTER EIGHT

The Wrath Of God

"For the wrath of God is revealed from heaven against all ungodliness and unrighteousness of men, who by their unrighteousness suppress the truth." (Romans 1:18 ESV)

The truth is truth *about* God. Having departed from Godliness and righteousness, people suppress the truth about God: that God is their loving Creator, and they are the created. Therefore, He deserves their worship and praise. Sinful people can mentally perceive the revealed truth of God (see verses 19-20), but they have chosen to *suppress* it. Therefore, they are without excuse!

RELIGION WITHOUT SALVATION

The overall purpose of this writing is to focus on those who think they are fine with God because they have familiarity with Christian things.

Do not flatter yourselves of being good enough, because you are morally so; because you go to church, say the prayers, and take the sacrament, therefore you think no more is required; alas, you are deceiving your own souls.   – George Whitfield

WARNING AGAINST FALSE PROPHETS

Jesus warned His followers to "remain on you guard for false prophets who come to you in sheep's clothing but inwardly are ravaging wolves" (see Matthew 7:15). Additionally, Jude urgently warns an unknown community of Christians against false prophets. Whether Jude is dependent on 2 Peter or Peter was dependent on Jude as in 2 Peter or a third some inter dependence is obvious. As in 2 Peter,

- these would be leaders are sensual (vv. 4, 16, 18),
- they pervert the truth (v. 4),
- and they are destined for divine judgment (vv. 14, 15).
- They are called "dreamers" in verse 8,
- They are "clouds without water" (v. 12),
- They are exposed as "not having the Spirit" in (v. 19).

Verse 19 alludes that these false teachers represented themselves as those who did have the Spirit (see Matthew 7:22, 23). Burk Parsons reminds Christians that "false teachers creep into the local church not because they look like false teachers but because they look like angels."

JUDE ADMONISHES THE CHRISTIANS TO GROW IN GODLINESS

There have always been those who attempt to draw local churches away from their main purpose. Whether angels or humans, God knows how to deal with the rebellious, but we are warned *not to* participate with any such persons. The wicked appeals to the lusts of the eye, lusts of the flesh, and the pride of life. They pretend to love God, appear to do good works, but a closer look reveals they are as fruitless as the fig tree Jesus cursed.

The wise will be able to discern through the Spirit those whose object is to *be* God rather than to serve God. We know that it is only by the working and grace of God that anyone is able to come joyfully into his presence in blameless worship. He is the lawful Ruler of every life.

WARNING AGAINST FALSE TEACHERS

Jude warns and appealing to you to <u>contend for the faith that was once for all delivered to the saints.</u> For certain people have *crept in unnoticed* who long ago were designated for this condemnation, ungodly people, who pervert the grace into sensuality and deny our only Master and Lord, Jesus Christ. (v.4)

Now I want to remind you, although you once fully knew it, that Jesus, who saved a people out of the land of Egypt, afterward destroyed those who did not believe. (v. 5)

False teachers often dig deep into a local church community and can pose a serious threat to the church by manipulating and misguiding people. Scripture warns that false teachers:

- create division (Romans 16:17)
- deceive with flattery (Romans 16:18)
- appease people by *departing* from sound doctrine (2 Timothy 4:3)
- destroy the standards and lead people astray (Matthew 24:11-13)
- take people captive through bad philosophy, bad theology, and bad psychology (Colossians 2:8)
- seem to have spiritual power and authority to deceive even the elect (Matthew 24:24)
- are bringing upon themselves a swift destruction (2 Peter 2:1)

THE HYPOCRITE

The hypocrite is the person who wears the mask of a Christian, so that he or she is seen and admired by others, but in actuality they have no desire to follow or worship Christ.

Hear His words:

"And when you pray, you must not be like the hypocrites.
For they love to stand and pray in the synagogues and at the

> *street corners, that they may be seen of others. Truly, I say, to you, they have received their reward. But when you pray, go into your room and shut the door and pray to your Father who is in secret. And your Father who sees in secret will reward you."* (Matthew 6:5-6 ESV)

This individual is external, and only concerned with covering self with veneer of public virtue. While the false prophet works to deceive others to a false gospel; the hypocrite seeks to deceive others for their own pride and appearance before the people. Like the Pharisees of Jesus' day, the individuals have an elitist view of their own morality, but they are unmistakably missing the fruit of a heart transformed by God. Be alert! One more thing, from the words of Jesus we read:

> *"Not everyone who says to me, "Lord, Lord, will enter the kingdom of heaven, but the one who does the will of my Father who is in heaven. On that day many will say to me, Lord, Lord, did we not prophesy in your name, and cast out demons, in your name, and do many mighty works in your name? And then I will declare to them, 'I never knew you; depart from me, you workers of lawlessness."* (Matthew 7:21-23 ESV)

CULTURAL CHRISTIANS

Cultural Christians are those who genuinely believe they are in good standing with God, because of church familiarity, a generic moral code, right political affiliation, and the right fraternal connections. It has been said, Cultural Christianity is largely based on *confusion,* whereas the false teacher and hypocrite have a Christianity based on *deceit.* There is so much more at stakes, since the cultural Christian take their ques from and conforms to the culture. They compromise with the culture's religious convictions and depart from the faith and biblical witness. Certainly the world does not need more conformity; it needs to be transformed. They need to hear the Word of God, from outside of itself. They need to hear and see Truth.

The power of culture is like a strong magnet which draws people back into the kingdoms of this world.   – Jay Leach

---

SELF-IDENTIFIED CHRISTIANS

Being a self-identified Christian for *cultural reasons,* rather than the *good news of the gospel* is commonplace in America today. This widespread complacency and biblical ignorance should be a wake-up call to the church. If asked about their *faith,* they would not feel uncomfortable, but answers would be about going to church and being good people. Church is a place where *basic* social expectations are met in the name of morals, family, and tradition. This is understandable, since the idea of church *isn't* linked much to belief in Jesus Christ or any demand the Scriptures would place on those who claim to be Christians.

To many self-identified Christians, it is very important that they be viewed as good people, the way they portray themselves on social media. They certainly believe in God and, as far as they are concerned, they always will. This person is defensive about their beliefs. But if the conversation moves to questions about Jesus, salvation and the gospel, that's another story. Many nod and smile, but soon they'd feel awkward because they would have no idea about what any of those questions about Jesus and the gospel have to do with them *personally.* They already see themselves a Christians. "Salvation" is something for extreme people, the religious type. Something very deep and dangerous to their awkwardness in a theological conversation makes it very difficult to present the gospel: the tragic reality is they don't believe they actually need Jesus. They have had plenty of exposure to Christian language, they were at the recent annual Easter Sunday service, they know about Jesus, and their faith is important to them. Sadly, such people are Christians without Christ.

FOLKS THIRSTY FOR SPIRITUALITY

The meaning and context of spirituality and religion have undergone a paradigm shift no less fundamental. The idea of God now allows for polytheism (many gods) or pantheism (a god identical with the universe). The average millennial or Gen Z in America today, no longer defines *a normal Christian life as knowledge of and communion with the infinite-yet-personal Creator and Lord of heaven and earth who is revealed in the Bible.* Spirituality has become a combination of do-it-yourself life games that blend ancient Eastern practices with modern consumerism.[9] My motivation for writing this book is out of deep concern to help explain the nature of this ongoing transformation and its effects within contemporary North American culture, which succeeds Western cultures of the Fifties. Even though prior to the 1960's culture of earlier times in the Western civilization has gone through a transformation of beliefs. While those cultures were just as sinful, and suffered many institutional problems, they existed under a basic worldview. Although people broke the rules, everyone was assuming basically the same rules. So that fundamental ideas about God, morality, marriage and family, motherhood, fatherhood, spirituality and religion were understood from a Christian perspective.

CHANGED RULES

The rules of engagement have changed right before our eyes. The *old* "prayer covering" of a basic Christian worldview, in our time has been blown apart and replaced by a *new* overarching body of beliefs and practices. Many of the traditional and true Christian structures that gave life meaning and significance under Christian influence in this country and the rest of Western civilization are morphed today:

- Marriage and the family are often functionally indistinguishable from mutually convenient cohabitation.
- Motherhood is celebrated in the same breath with abortion on demand.
- Morality is relativized by various (and often contradictory) personal or social convictions.
- Honesty means being true to one's inner commitments and longing for more stuff.

---

[9] Accessed 8/2/24. https:en:wikpedia. Org./wiki/consumerism. Communism is a social and economic order in which appropriations of many individuals to include the acquisition of goods and services beyond those necessary for survival or traditional displays of status.

Perhaps there will be those who read this book who are not as old as I am and who still have enough youthful optimism to believe you can pour new wine into old wineskins. I no longer hold that view. The hope of the church is in the formation of new wineskins. No matter how rich and tasty the wine may be, if it leaks out all over the ground, what good is it?

Jay Leach

STUDY GUIDE: CHAPTER 8 THE WRATH OF GOD

1. The truth is truth about _____.

2. Sinful people can mentally perceive the _____ _____ of God.

3. Jesus warned His followers to remain ___ _____ _____ for false prophets who come to you in _____ _____ but inwardly are ravaging _____.

4. The wise will be able to discern through the Spirit those whose object is to be _____ rather than to _____ God.

5. A _____ is the person who _____ the mask of a _____.

6. Cultural Christians are those who genuinely believe they are in good standing with _____ because of church _____.

7. Church is a place where basic social expectations are met in the name of _____, _____, and _____.

SECTION THREE

GET RIGHT
OR
GET LEFT

CHAPTER NINE

Biblical Discipleship Is Not Optional

And there went great multitudes with him and he turned and said unto them. *"If any man come to me, and hate not his father, and mother, and children, and brethren and sisters, yea, and his own life also, he **cannot** be my disciple. And whosoever doth not bear his cross and come after me, **cannot** be my disciple. For which of you, intending to build a tower, sitteth not down first, and counteth the cost, whether he have sufficient to finish it? Lest haply, after he hath laid the foundation, and is not able to finish it, all that behold it began to mock him. Saying, this man began to build, and was not able to finish it all. Or what king, going against another, sitteth not down first, and consulteth whether he be able to meet him with a thousand to meet him that cometh against him with twenty thousand? Or else, while the other is yet a great way off, he sendeth an ambassage, and desireth conditions of peace. So likewise,* *whosoever he be of you that forsaketh not all that he hath, he* **cannot** *be my disciple."* (Luke 14:25-33 KJV).

CONTINUED SPIRITUAL GROWTH

We are not only saved from sin, but also saved to a lifetime commitment to Christ within a new body of believers. This is grand, but for a new believer, it can be overwhelming. It is vitally important that all local churches focus in on caring for those sheep new to the flock and make sure they are able to understand the new life they have in *Christ*. The answer to encroaching *error* is steadfastness through growing in the knowledge of the Lord. Some practical ways the local church can bring people into the fold for continued spiritual growth:

BIBLE READING

In his book *The Shape of Faith to Come*, Brad Waggoner, the number one indicator of spiritual growth is regular Bible reading.[10] According to a Lifeway survey presented by Ed Stetzer,[11] those who engage in Bible reading are more likely to:

- Confess sins to God and ask forgiveness.
- Decide to follow God realizing that to do so can be costly.
- Pray for spiritual state of people they know are not professing Christians.
- Read a book about increasing their spiritual growth.
- Be discipled one by one by a more spiritually matured person.[12]

Stetzer adds that "Bible engagement points people toward maturity, and maturing Christians have practices that correspond to Bible

---

[10] Brad J. Waggoner, *The Shape of Things to Come: Spiritual Formation and the Future of Discipleship* (Nashville: B&H, 2008) 78

[11] Ed Stetzer, "Bible Engagement Impacts Spiritual Maturity," Facts and Trends, June 12, 2013, https://factsandtrends.net/2013/06/12/bible-engagement-impacts-spiritual-maturity/.

[12] Ibid.

Reading." This must accompany a heavy reliance on Scripture during the church service itself, in order to give as much exposure to God's Word as possible.

At Bread of Life Ministries, we offer open seminars, discipleship training, and access to our Bread of Life Bible Institute. If a church can offer environments for people to come together and learn, you may find that they are excited about doing so. For our church these environments also allow our people to come together and fellowship outside of the structure of a normal Sunday gathering.

SERVICE

Service is a continuing subject in the teachings of Jesus. It was a virtue[13] of importance to Him and He practiced it. [Virtue is no longer found in Cultural Christianity's societal dictionary]. If Jesus was a man who lived to serve others, then certainly the church is [His Body] as it exists for others in the practice of agape love.

Following Jesus is joining Him in the service of humanity. Throughout His teachings are the recurrent themes of the necessity and the dignity of service [acts of worship]. In his book: *"Dissident Discipleship,"* David Augsburger lists many such Scriptural themes Jesus used that all of us should adhere to:

- There are great servants (see Mark 10:44; Luke 22:26).
- To lead is to serve (see Mark 10:44; Matthew 6:24).
- It is in caring for the other that we find our true calling (see Mark 10:45; Luke 22:27).
- It is in serving that we become rich (Luke 16:13; Matthew 6:24).
- It is in giving that we receive, in losing our life that we find it (see John 12:24-26).
- To serve a child is to serve God (see Mark 9:36-37).
- Service nourishes humility; dominance feeds arrogance (see Matthew23:11; Luke 22:24-27; Matthew:25-28).
- Friendship is availability and openness to mutual service (see John 15:13-17).[14]

---

[13] According to Webster's New Students Dictionary (1964), Virtue is used to signify intrinsic value, moral excellence, and goodness.

[14] David Augsburger, *Dissident Discipleship* Brazos Press 2006).

GENERAL PRAYERS

Concerning situations in life, we often hear people say, "just let it go." It's easy to say, but what does it mean to "let it go?" Does it mean just to drop it, or does mean you have to deposit your fear, worry, or problem into God's hands, trusting Him to take care of it and bring it to fulfillment? This is a decision you not only have to make, *but then keep.* This is the hard part.

The reason it is so hard is because we don't really trust God to do it. For example, our desire may be for our husband or wife to go to church, and we think, "If I don't lecture him/her about it, remind them, and *put them on a guilt trip, who will?"* But deep down do we trust God to nudge them? Do we trust the Holy Spirit to guide, draw, and convict, or do we know how to do it better than God?

Your spouse should never hear you nag or complain, and definitely never lecture. In spite of what you think about them like, they are stupid, careless, inconsiderate, lazy, but not only should those words never come out of your mouth regarding your spouse – you should never even think them. *Love conquers all, heals all, and saves all.* Love is triumphant and so are you when you *choose* to follow Christ and "lay it down." Watch God do the work.

What are your fears, worries, concerns, and problems? Are your adult children addicted or away from God, are you afraid of losing your job, unemployed, an illness, marital problems? How do we get to the place where we can "lay it down." Define your problem and write it down:

"Help me prayers" are good when you are a baby Christian or desperate, but you will find that God is growing you up and out of that prayer. Ask! Over and over God tells us to ask. Ask believing that God is listening and wants to answer your prayers.

BELIEVING PRAYERS

Prayer without faith is really no prayer. It's time to bring our prayers to the next level (Proclaim): This is for those of you ready to grow and mature and see breakthrough. "Proclaim" is speaking out loud the answer to your prayer as if it has already been answered. This is critical. In Mark 11 Jesus says, *"Have faith in God … whatever you ask for in prayer, believe that you have received it, and it will be yours."* (Mark 11:24 ESV)

Proclaim Example: My son is seeking the Lord. I have faith in God. My son is walking in wisdom and grace and is full of the Holy Spirit and free from drugs in the name of Jesus.

This is your way of showing God that you believe you have received what you asked for. Faith and trust are important to God. When we say "I am well" we are saying it not because we feel or look well but because we believe God heard our prayer and is doing something about it. Our **faith** is now on God because we just prayed. It is *in essence faith in our prayer.* It shows God you really believe He is healing you.

When I say "I am well in the name of Jesus" I believe that He is working, and I am choosing to **walk by faith and not by sight** (see 2 Corinthians 5:7). I also believe in the **power of His name,** and I am coming to Him in the name of Jesus. This is hard at first but **so powerful,** for instance, when Magdalene and I asked God to heal our son and deliver him from drugs, certainly, we wanted to do it without complaining to family, or friends just how bad he really was. This was our time. Just because we couldn't see Him, we prayed. **Have you pray? Don't you believe God is doing something?** Though we could not see Him, we believed He was working, healing, and delivering our son? God did it! We continue thank and praise Him for it! He went through no programs, and he has not suffered any relapse – that was 35 years ago. He is married and enjoys a godly family life. He has a fine home and business. There are no identifiable aftershocks. God did it! The woman with the issue of blood said, "If I only just touch His garment, I will be well (Mark 5:28). The stretcher bearers said, "If only we can get him to Jesus," and they went in through the roof. The centurion said, "Just speak the word." It's time to stop talking like God isn't working or He didn't hear you. Have **faith.** Show you have faith by what comes out of your mouth. For example, speak it! My son is seeking the Lord. I have faith in God.

Proclaim Example: My son/ daughter is walking in wisdom and grace and is full of the Holy Spirit and free from drugs or (something else) in the name of Jesus. Every time we declare or proclaim:

1. It reminds us that we have prayed.
2. It reminds us that we have "laid it down."
3. It reminds us that God is working on our behalf and answering the prayer.
4. It's a reminder that we are trusting God.

It's our declaration and proclamation that proves to us and to God that we laid it down and let it go. It takes time and effort and a decision to lay it down. Our proclamation reminds us we prayed and proves our faith to God that we believe He heard us and is doing something. Our proclamation is showing God, we trust in Him and have more faith in Him than what it looks like. Declare it *every day,* and you will be reminded that you have prayed, and now it's up to God. Every time you declare it you will be reminded you prayed. I prayed for this, and I am confident God is working it out.

So now speak your prayer back to God as if it has been done.

> *"Jesus said to them in reply. 'Have faith in God, Amen, I say to you, whoever says to this mountain. 'Be lifted up and thrown into the sea, 'and does not doubt in his heart but believes that what he says will happen, it shall be done for him [or her]. Therefore, I tell you, all that you ask for in prayer, believe that you receive it, and it shall be yours"* (Mark 11:22-24)

You just believe in something that hasn't manifested in the physical realm yet. The Bible says that faith comes by hearing. Every time you declare it you hear it.

UNITY

One picture of the church likens it to the human body. Christ is the Head. The Holy Spirit immerses each new believer into the body, properly connected at conversion as a working, functional member. Paul explains in 1 Corinthians 12:14-19 that the unity of this body is such that one body part never says, "I have no need of you" to another member. As the hand and foot and stomach must interact, even so the members of the body of Christ must live intimacy. The members are united into a whole. There is freedom from diversity, a *oneness* of mind or feelings, exactly like that of a human body. The concept of bodily parts is responsible for building up one another becomes the focus of their lifestyle (see Ephesians 4:15-16).

In Mark 1:19 the Greek word is translated *"equipping"* in Ephesians 4:12: each body member is to participate in helping other body members be repaired for service. In Galatians 6:1 the *"spiritual ones"* are described as mending other body parts that are damaged (restoring to ministry).

In a study of the early church, one observes that this is theory which was put into practice without a great amount of instruction. Paul describes the mutual building up of believers in 1 Corinthians 14. His order is for every single Christian to use spiritual gifts for the purpose of building up the church. He scoffs at the idea of exercising gifts for personal enjoyment. The word *oikodomeo*, appears six times in his teaching (verses 3, 4, 5, 12, 17, 26) as he bears down on the fact that *each one* (absolutely no exceptions!) is to participate in the ministry of building the body: "When you assemble *each one* has a psalm, has a teaching, has a revelation, has a tongue, or has an interpretation. Let all things be done for edification (building up)."

The word for "each one" used here does not mean, "each one of you who desires to enter into ministry," but "every single person in the group is to be a participant in the building up." Physical nor spiritual youthfulness should not be reasons for exemption from participating. All are to exercise spiritual gifts to edify others. But if all prophesy, and an unbeliever or an ungifted man enters, he is convicted by *all;* he is called to account by *all;* the secrets of his heart are disclosed; and so he will fall on his face and worship God, declaring that God is certainly among you (see 1 Corinthians 14:24-25).

SPIRITUAL MATURITY

Our Lord knows there are two factors in *spiritual growth. One* is receiving His *power;* the other is becoming the *channel* of that power. Spiritual maturity only occurs when both are experienced. The greatest men and women among the early churches were those who served, not those who led. The *power* of the Spirit through the church is the most important feature in the book of Acts.

The Work of the Holy Spirit in Acts cannot be understood without seeing the relationship between Acts and the Gospels, which demonstrates the importance of continuity between the two. Both Jesus' public ministry in the Gospels and the public ministry of the church in Acts begin with a life-changing event with the Holy Spirit; together both accounts are necessary of the results of that event.

The power of the Spirit in Jesus' life ordained Him to preach the kingdom of God and to demonstrate power by healing the sick, casting out demons, and setting the captives free (see Luke 4:14-19; Matthew 4:23). The same Spirit *power* in Acts 2 gave the same authority to the disciples.

Jesus is the prototype of the Spirit-filled, Spirit-empowered life (Acts 10:38).

Luke's terminology in describing the experiences of the people with the Holy Spirit in Acts is moving. He notes that people were "filled with the Holy Spirit" (Acts 2;4; 9:17), that "they received the Holy Spirit" (8:17), that "the Holy Spirit fell upon them" (10:44), that "the Holy Spirit had been poured out on [them]" (10:45), and that "the Holy Spirit came upon them" (19:6). These occurrences are all equivalents of Jesus' promise that the church would "be baptized with the Holy Spirit" (1:5; the immediate fulfillment in (2:4).

In the Old Testament only those called or anointed of God received the Holy Spirit. But under the New Covenant every believer is given the promise of the Father (Luke 24:49), the active indwelling presence of the Holy Spirit. By the activity of the Spirit's fulness in the life of every believer, dynamic devotion is possible, and the ministry of Christ in His church continues.

GROWTH IN THE SPIRIT

John's Gospel introduces the Holy Spirit's role in spiritual growth. The New Birth and the baptism with the Holy Spirit endowing the believer with the life and gifts of the Holy Spirit, including the ability to pray in the Spirit power. The Holy Spirit is our Teacher, Helper, Advocate, and Guide. He is our source of true spiritual understanding. He lifts up Jesus and builds up believers, enabling them to live the Christian life. Acts 1:8 is the key verse to the book of Acts!

STUDY GUIDE: CHAPTER 9
DISCIPLESHIP IS NOT OPTIONAL

1. We are not only saved from sin, but also saved to a lifetime commitment to Christ within a new body of believers.

2. The answer to growing *error* is steadfastness through growing in the _____ of the _____.

3. From the text list three practical ways the local church can bring people into the fold for continued spiritual growth to maturity:

    1.
    2.
    3.

4. If Jesus was a man who lived to serve others, then certainly the church is [His Body] as it exists for others in the practice of *agape love*.

5. In prayer, what does it mean "to just let it go?"

6. How do we get to the place where we can "lay it down."

7. Stop talking like God isn't working or He didn't hear your prayer – just have faith!

CHAPTER TEN

Why Is Disciple-Making Ignored In The Local Church?

"Go therefore and make disciples of all the nations, baptizing them in the name of the Father and of the Son and of the Holy Spirit, 'teaching them to observe all things that I have commanded you; and lo, I am with you always, even to the end of the age." Amen. (Matthew 28:19-20)

Matthew presents Jesus as the Lord and Teacher of the church, the new community, which is called to *live out* the new ethic of the kingdom of heaven. Jesus declares "the church" as His choice instrument for fulfilling the purposes of God on earth (see Matthew 16:18; 18:15-20). It's possible Matthew's gospel may have served as a teaching manual for the early church, including the dynamic world-oriented Great Commission (28:12-20).

Earlier, Jesus used the occasion of the Passover meal to inaugurate the New Covenant. The symbolism of the Passover meal under the Old Covenant was about to be fully satisfied through Christ's crucifixion. In this historic moment, Jesus transformed the meaning of the elements of the Passover meal into New Covenant thought.

The bread now represented His body, which would be given, and the cup His blood, which would be shed for the forgiveness of sins. The holy requirements of God and the Old Covenant were about to be forever satisfied. A new and living way into the presence and provision of God was being prepared through Christ, the Lamb of God. A new and eternal bond was being established by the blood of Jesus Christ. God was sovereignly inaugurating the new and ultimate covenant (see Jerimiah 31:31-33).

The content of the apostles' future teaching will be from what Jesus had *commanded* them. Jesus assures them of His constant presence as they go on their *divinely* commanded mission. While Jesus' ministry had been to Israel (see 10:5, 6), the proclamation of and adherence to His Lordship is extended *to all nations* through the Spirit-empowered ministry of His church (see Acts1:7, 8).

Disciples are to acknowledge openly their allegiance to Christ by the seal of water baptism, which is ministered under the authority of the entire Godhead.

THE LOCAL CHURCH

I read a great story about Dawson Trotman. In the early 1930s, Trotman, a young lumberyard worker, became inspired by 2 Timothy 2:2: *"What you have heard from me in the presence of many witnesses entrust to faithful men who will be able to teach others also."* He began teaching high school students *to disciple one another,* and then, in 1933, extended this work to the United States Navy, founding a group called The Navigators. He mentored one sailor, who in turn *mentored* many more on board the USS *West Virginia*. Before the ship sank at Pearl Habor, 125 men were growing in Christ and sharing their faith. During World War II, The Navigators ministry spread to thousands in the United States Navy on ships and bases around the world.

The Navigators continued working in the growing military population until 1951 when they also began to work with college students on the campus of the University of Nebraska. Trotman died in 1956 rescuing a young girl from drowning in upstate New York. But the work went on. Today hundreds of college campuses around the world have a Navigators group *evangelizing* and *discipling students.* The Navigators website describes the organization as "a ministry that helps people grow in Jesus Christ as they navigate through life." They also say, "We spread the Good News of Jesus Christ by establishing life-on-life mentoring or discipling – relationships with people, equipping them to make an impact on those around them for God's glory.

Some people raise concerns about ministries like The Navigators, and our very own Bread of Life Ministries replacing the church. *Para* means *beside.* In many cases, the ministry has to move on.

If it is unwise to do discipling without a church, it's worse to do church without discipling.

Isn't that the case with many local churches? Christians join churches, and no one comes alongside them. In fact, to many local churches today, discipling is antiquated and their program does not have time nor space for it. In such churches there is no one to:

- Come alongside them.
- There is no culture of single folks.
- There is little hospitality.
- There are no husbands or older men discipling the younger men and boys.
- There are no wives or older women discipling the younger women and girls.
- There are no men shepherding their wives.
- No thought of helping a family or marriage in trouble.
- Counseling only happens in offices.
- Few young men.
- No reaching out to people with a different skin color or accent.

Yet, the gathered local church is responsible to preach the whole counsel of God through those who are spiritually gifted for this purpose. Through baptism the local church affirms the converts salvation experience. Through the Lord's Supper the church declares the Lord's death and resurrection making the many into *one*. And through excommunication it removes anyone whose life unrepentantly contradicts his or her profession.

The local church through the power of the Holy Spirit is the natural environment for discipling. It also teaches that the local church is itself the basic discipler of Christians. The church does this through its weekly gatherings and its accountability structures, which in turn provide the context for the one-on-one discipling we have put forth. Now that we have the church's skeletal structure, we can move on to relationships.

RELATIONSHIPS

Now we come to the area of relationships, which are like the flesh and muscle. In their life together, the *members* of a church practice loving one another as Jesus has loved them:

> *"A new commandment I give to you, that you love one another: just as I have loved you, you also are to love one another. By this all people will know that you are my disciples, if you have love for one another"* (John 13:34-35).

With what kind of love did Jesus love his disciples? He loved them with a love that continually pointed to the words of the Father: That demonstrated his love through obeying the Father. That assured them of a place being prepared for them. That ultimately laid down his life so that they could be forgiven. Where can we love like this?

We find it only in an environment where we can love by pointing to the words of the Father and the Son, by affirming repentance and baptism, by affirming that the many are one through the Supper, and by sacrificing our own agendas through forgiveness. In these most basic ways, the local church is the primary discipler of all Christians. Our churches will never be perfect; however, 1 Corinthians 13 implies that a local church should be a preview or foretaste of that world [Heaven].

A RULE OF ENGAGEMENT

The discipling work of the church begins with what I call – a rule of engagement first, by simply "gathering together." The author of Hebrews writes, *"And let us consider how to stir up one another to love and good works, not neglecting to meet together, as is the habit of some, but encouraging one another, and all the more as you see the Day drawing near."* (Hebrews 10:24-25 ESV)

Notice the goal here is to help "one another" follow Jesus, or, as Hebrews puts it, stir up one another to love and good works. The Millennials and Gen Zers [who love to see action on the Word] are interested in the "one another "ministries. There are some fifty "one another statements and commands" in the New Testament which call us to a special kind of life together as (disciples):

The following statements and commands are in the NIV:

- "Be at peace with one another" (Mark 9:50).
- "Wash one another's feet" (John 13:U14).
- "Love one another" (John18:34).
- "Love one another" (13:35).
- "Love one another" (15:12).
- "Love one another" (15:17).
- "Be devoted to one another in brotherly love" (Romans 12:10).
- "Honor one another above yourselves" (Romans 12:10).
- "Love in harmony with one another" (Romans 12:16).
- "Love one another" (Romans 13:8).
- "Stop passing judgment on one another" (Romans 14:13).
- "Accept one another, then, just as Christ accepted you" (Romans 15:7).
- "Instruct one another" (Romans 15:14).
- "Greet one another with a holy kiss" (Romans 16:16).
- "When you come together to eat, wait for one another" (1 Corinthians 11:33).
- "Have equal concern for one another" (1 Corinthians 12:25).
- "Greet one another with a holy kiss" (1 Corinthians 16:20).
- "Greet one another with a holy kiss" (2 Corinthians 13:12).
- "Serve one another in love" (Galatians 5:18).

- "If you keep on biting and devouring one another … you will be destroyed by each other" (Galatians 5:15).
- "Let us not become conceited, provoking and envying one another" (Galatians 5:26).

Barna survey results show that those 18-29 years old are more interested in the "one another" ministries than older generations.

- "Teach one another" (Colossians 3:16).
- "Admonish one another" (Colossians 3:16).
- "Make your love increase and overflow for one another" (1 Thessalonians 3:12).
- "Love one another" (1 Thessalonians 4:9).
- "Encourage one another" (1 Thessalonians 4:18).
- "Encourage one another" (1 Thessalonians 5:11).
- "Build up one another" (1 Thessalonians 5:11).
- "Exhort one another daily" (Hebrews 3:13).
- "Spur one another on toward love and good deeds" (Hebrews 10:24).
- "Encourage one another" (Hebrews 10:25).
- "Do not slander one another" (James 4:11).
- "Do not grumble against one another" (James 5:9).
- "Confess your sins to one another" (James 5:16).
- "Pray for one another" (James 5:16).
- "Love one another deeply from the heart" (1 Peter 1:22).
- "Live in harmony with one another" (1 Peter 3:8).
- "Love one another deeply" (1 Peter 4:8).
- "Offer hospitality to one another without grumbling" (1 Peter 4:9).
- "Each one should use whatever gift he or she has received to serve one another" (1 Peter 4:10).
- "Clothe yourself with humility toward one another" (1 Peter 5:5).
- "Greet one another with a kiss of love" (1 Peter 5:14).
- "Love one another" (1 John 3:11).
- "Love one another" (1 John 3:23).
- "Love one another" (1 John 4:7).

- "Love one another" (1 John 4:11).
- "Love one another" (1 John 4:12).
- "Love one another" (2 John 5).

It is obvious that these "one another ministries" operating in the local churches are very important to God, since He speaks of them so frequently in the Scriptures.

GATHERING TOGETHER

The church's discipling work begins quite simply by gathering together. The writer of Hebrews writes, *"And let us consider how to stir up one another to love and good works, not neglecting to meet together, as is the habit of some, but encouraging one another, and all the more as you see the Day drawing near.* (Hebrews 10:24-25 ESV)

The goal here is to help one another follow Jesus, or as the writer puts it, stir up one another to love and good works. And how does the author say a church accomplishes that goal? By **not neglecting** meeting together [gathering]. This is how we "encourage" one another. Regular gathering gives shape to following Jesus and helping others follow Jesus. Why then are the majority of local Churches in America neglecting this command/ministry? Why is it on the back burner?

In a culture afloat in a sea of outrage, and pain, the Christian's worldview frequently does not look very different from those around them who hold secular worldviews. We have the same addictions, play the same political games, reveal the same fears, and anxieties, as our neighbors, and coworkers. When our worldview is *markedly similar* to that of a person that doesn't know Jesus Christ, what does that say about the local church? The reality of Christ's:

- Redemptive work
- The indwelling of the Holy Spirit
- Our adoption as coheirs in the kingdom of God

should present a very different worldview. However, Christians too often appear *conformed*. Instead of appearing changed and renewed. Since you have heard about Jesus and learned the truth that comes from him some Christians feel challenged. We need to hear Paul's exhortation:

But that isn't what you learned about Christ. Since you have heard about Jesus and have learned the truth that came from him, throw off your old sinful nature and your former way of life, which is corrupted by lust and deception. Instead, let the Spirit renew your thoughts and attitudes. Put on your new nature, created to be like God – truly righteous and holy. (Ephesians 4:20-24 NLT)

Scripture warns us about the quality of voices we allow into our lives. We must develop the input and output for our lives that will shape our world according to God's truth. What we see and hear is depicted as the gateway to what we love and worship. The Psalmist outlines the way Scripture *guides* and protects us against sin. We should prayerfully study Paul's list in Philippians 4:8 ("Whatever is true, whatever is noble, whatever is right, whatever is pure, whatever is lovely, whatever is admirable – if anything is excellent, or praiseworthy." (NIV)

Paul offers himself as an example, for his effort had been not only to teach Christianity – but to display it in his own walk and life-living. His readers in past, present, and future generations may be sure of this protection when their one aim is to do what is right, and to be steadfast to their Christian faith.

STUDY GUIDE: CHAPTER 10 WHY IS DISCIPLE-MAKING IGNORED?

1. Matthew presents Jesus as _____ and _____ of the church, the new community, which is called to _____ _____ the new ethic of the kingdom of heaven.

2. Jesus used the occasion of the Passover meal to inaugurate the New Covenant.

3. Jesus transformed the meaning of the elements of the Passover meal into New Covenant thought. The *bread* now represented His body, which would be given, and the *cup* His blood, which would be shed for the forgiveness of sins.

4. To many local churches, _____ is antiquated and the program does not have _____ nor _____ for it.

5. The local church through the power of the Holy Spirit is the _____ environment for discipling.

6. In their life together, the members of a church _____ _____ one another as Jesus has _____ them.

7. We find this love only in an environment where we can love by pointing to the words of the Father and the Son, by affirming repentance and baptism, by affirming that the many are one through the supper, and by sacrificing our own agendas through forgiveness.

CHAPTER ELEVEN

It Takes A Disciple To Make A Disciple

"And what you have heard from me in the presence of many witnesses entrust to faithful men, who will be able to teach also." (2 Timothy 2:2 ESV)

There is a contagion about the Christian faith and life. Young people are won to Christ and belief in the first instance by coming in contact with people in whose lives Christian faith and convictions are realities. But Christianity must also *be taught*. Part of the commandment of Jesus was to *love God with the mind*.

Christians must be ready to give a reason for **the faith** that is in them!

An intelligent member of the Christian church should know the history of Christianity, what it teaches, how great Christians have answered some of its basic questions, and how the faith has spread, and what it has accomplished in the world. One of the weaknesses of the local churches in America is Christians have not been taught in their faith.

In our text above Paul pleads for a succession of the teachers (disciples), passing on Christian knowledge from generation to generation, as runners in a relay race pass the torch or the wand. Paul has taught (discipled) Timothy, who is urged to teach other **faithful men, [and women],** who in turn are to teach (disciple), others.

In many of our churches there is a healthy emphasis on creative teaching which builds on the *actual experience* of the learner, who learns by doing. This is not exclusive of nor a substitute for transmission of Christian knowledge from life to life. Because every local church has its problems in recruiting and training people as disciples. Note Paul's suggestions in the matter:

Christian disciple-making disciples are to be *first* of all those **willing,** to learn what is committed to them. *Second,* they must be **faithful,** an indispensable quality, as every disciple-maker knows. *Third,* they must be **able.** No enthusiasm for the task can take the place of genuine capacity, and the teaching (discipling) task of the church is so important that it should command the services of the ablest. *Fourth,* they must be concerned about **others also,** eager to share with others what means most to them and be zealous to present every man perfect in Christ.

WHAT IT MEANS TO BE A CHRISTIAN DISCIPLE

Paul uses three metaphors (see vv. 3-7), as illustrations of what it means to be a Christian disciple. Like a **soldier,** he or she must be ready to **endure hardships.** Like an **athlete,** he or she must follow the **rules.** Like a **farmer,** he or she must **work hard** to get results.

- Having seen that it is possible for good men to fall away, Timothy is urged to remember the **source of power in Christ Jesus.** The admonition in (2:2) to true loyalty and devotion to the received Christian faith are driven home in verses 3-6 by three illustrations stress the fact that if one wants to achieve success in any profession, he or she must devotedly themself to it completely. Paul is thought of as indeed the most distinguished example of those who have suffered, but suffering is expected

It Is Finished

of **every good soldier of Christ Jesus.** The term good soldier, here in the New Testament, military metaphors however, are common, for example, the armor of God in Ephesians 6:10-17. The soldier has always stood as the model of unhesitating obedience, of perfect loyalty, of single-minded and heroic devotion, and of the ultimate in self-sacrifice. It is these virtues which are transformed to the realm of spirit in the phrase **a good soldier of Christ Jesus.**

- The professional **athlete** who breaks the rules is disqualified. Again the application of the metaphor, disciple (learner) is in detail not clear. The **rules** may be taken as meaning: (a) those by which the contest is actually waged, or (b) those which specify the nature and extent of the preliminary training. He or she knows what the requirements are; let them whole-heartedly obey them.

- Although the stress have is clearly and wholly on the **hard-working farmer,** the third illustration appears less impressive than the other two because of the concern with the personal reward due the farmer. It is true reward or recompense is assumed in the military and athletic figures: the soldier with livelihood; the athlete is crowned. Yet in neither case is the idea of personal gain so prominent as in (vs. 6). However, strict parallelism of illustration would have called for something like "A farmer who does not work will not get good crops, or "it is only a hard-working farmer who deserves success." The awkwardness of the present text may be due to the fact that the agricultural metaphor was so consistently used in the church as defense of the right of the minister to claim support from the laity (see 1 Timothy; 1 Corinthians 9:3-14) that it could scarcely be bent to any other purpose.

- To be a Christian means to be a Christian disciple. There are no Christians who are not disciples. And to be a disciple of Jesus means to follow Jesus. There are no disciples of Jesus who are not following Him. Checking the box on an opinion poll, or sincerely labeling yourself with the religion of you parents, or just as a religious preference. Evangelist Billy Graham illustrated this in a sermon: "Sleeping in a garage overnight does not make you an automobile."

- Christian disciples are people who have real faith in the Lord, Jesus Christ and who show it by resting their hopes, fears, and lives entirely upon Him. They follow Him wherever He leads them. You no longer set your agenda for your own life; Jesus Christ does that. You belong to Him now. "You are not your own," Paul says, "You were bought with a price" (see 1 Corinthians 6:19-20). Jesus is not just our Savior; He is our Lord.

- Paul explains, "And he died for all, that those who live should no longer live for themselves but for him who died for them and was raised again" (2 Cor. 5:15 NIV). So Christian discipleship begins right here with the acceptance of the free gift: grace, mercy, a relationship with God and a promise of life eternal. Through faith we turn away from sin and follow Him.

A STUIDED ROUTINE

The Word of God, the Bible is the only conclusive source of wisdom, knowledge, and understanding concerning fundamental and final realities. It is a fountainhead of freeing truth (see John 8:32), and a gold mine of practical principles (Psalm 19:10), waiting to liberate and enrich the person who will pursue its *truth* and *wealth*. Thus, Paul's instruction to *"be diligent … a worker"* has been applied by serious Christians through the centuries as a directive to study the Word of God.

As noted earlier, the only way to healthy, balanced Christian living is through the *"rightly dividing"* (Greek *orthotomounta*, literally, *"cutting straight"*) of God's Word. Such correct, straight-forward application of God's Word is the result of diligent study. The text calls us beyond the casual approaches to the Scriptures, telling us to refuse to adjust the Bible to our own convenience, ideology, and age – but we are to adjust the age to the Bible.

In his earlier words (1 Timothy 4:13) Paul also told Timothy, *"Give to reading God's Word,"* but now he emphasizes *studying* like a "worker" (from Greek *ergon* – "toil, effort"). Psalms 119:11 urges memorizing the Word of God as a deterrent against sin. Memorizing the Scripture also provides an immediate availability of God's "words" as a ready *sword* in **witnessing:**

*For the word of God is living and **powerful**, and sharper than any two-edged sword, piercing even to the division of soul and spirit, and of joints and marrow, and is a discerner of the thoughts and intents of the heart.* (Hebrews 4:12)

And the word of God **powerful** in **spiritual warfare:**

*Finally, my brethren, be strong in the Lord and in the **power** of His might.* (Ephesians 6:10)

Yes, Paul admonishes us to put on the whole armor of God in order to stand against the forces of hell. It is clear that our warfare is not against physical forces, but against *invisible powers* who have clearly defined levels of authority in a real, through invisible, sphere of activity.

Paul not only warns us of a clearly defined structure in the invisible realm; he instructs us to take up the whole armor of God in order to maintain a "battle stance" against this unseen satanic structure. All of this armor is not just a passive protection in facing the enemy; it is used offensively against these satanic forces.

Then, note Paul's final instructions: we are to be *"praying always with all prayer and supplication in the Spirit"* (v. 18). Thus, prayer is not so much a weapon, or even a part of the armor, as it is a *means* by which we engage in the battle itself and the purpose for which we are armed.

To put on the armor of God is to prepare for battle. [We will cover this subject more in depth in Chapter 16-18]. Prayer is the battle itself, with God's Word being our chief weapon employed against Satan during our struggle. God's Word: Read it! Study it! Memorize it! Live it!

AGAINST FLESH AND BLOOD

One of the church's greatest demands is to discern between the spiritual struggle and other social, personal, and political complexities. Otherwise, individual believers groups become to easily detoured, "wrestling" with human adversaries instead of prayerfully warring against the invisible works of hell behind the scenes.

STUDY GUIDE: CHAPTER 11 IT TAKES A DISCIPLE TO MAKE A DISCIPLE

1. There is a _____ about Christian faith and life.

2. One of the weaknesses of the local churches in America is _____ have not been _____ in their faith.

3. Part of the commandment of Jesus was to love God with all of your _____.

4. In our text Paul _____ for a succession of the _____ passing on Christian knowledge from _____ to _____.

5. Paul uses three metaphors (vv. 3-7) as illustrations of what it means to be a _____ _____.

6. The Word of God, the Bible is the only _____ source of wisdom, knowledge, and understanding concerning fundamental and _____ _____.

7. To put on the armor of God is to prepare for battle. _____ is the battle itself.

CHAPTER TWELVE

Shake The Dust Off Your Feet

And whosoever shall not receive you, nor hear your words,
when you depart out of that house or city,
shake off the dust of your feet.
– Matthew 10:14

The plan was detailed and set. The apostles were to inquire, as they entered a village, for people of like mind. If they found such a home, they were to ask for hospitality; and, if welcomed, they were to **abide** there, and not move from home to home. They were to **tell the good news,** finding through that home contact with others who might welcome the gospel. Such were the beginnings of the Christian missions. The disciples would be welcomed by worthy folks. The adjective means worthy in spirit and worthy to receive the gospel of Christ. The apostles were to announce **peace** to such as were in Christ; the benediction would bring peace – "waiting for the consolation of Israel." Elsewhere the disciples might be denied. Why?

- People with an "intellectual" mind might fear another heresy.
- People with a "stingy" mind might dislike hospitality.

- People seeking personal fame might decide it unwise to associate "with one of these new movements."
- People with iconoclastic minds might despise religion and plead for recourse by the sword.

In such cases the apostles were to **shake the dust from their feet.** This is what the Pharisees did when leaving "heathen" territory. But the disciples were not to do it in a Pharisaic mood. One early writer called this act "the Sacrament of Failure." Perhaps we need such a "sacrament"; today the Christian appeal meets denial and abuse. So the disciples were to perform this simple ritual, not in anger, not in pride, not in wounded irritation; but in love as those who are reaching the end of human power are content to leave all issues to the judgment of God. This judgment is sternly stated in verse 15:

> *Verily I say unto you, it shall be more tolerable for the land of Sodom and Gomorrah in the day of judgment, than for that city. KJV*

Some commentators think this is quite stiff, and that Sodom and Gomorrah could plead for some measure of ignorance. But the Jews had been prepared through centuries for the revealing of God. Their judgments remained! Privilege always equates to responsibility. While the applications of that truth are numerous today – they rest most heavily on the church.

"Privilege always equates to responsibility!"

Do you accept the fact, that it's your responsibility to help build and maintain a healthy church if you are a Christian? We believe that it is.

- Jesus commands you to make disciples (Matthew 28:18-20).
- Jude says to build yourself up in the faith (Jude vv. 20-21).
- Peter calls you to use your spiritual gifts to serve others (1 Peter 4:10).
- Paul tells you to speak the truth in love so that your church will become mature (Ephesians 4:13, 15).

Local churches exist to display God's glory to the nations. We do that by fixing our eyes on the gospel of Jesus Christ, trusting Him for salvation, and then loving one another with God's own holiness, unity, and love. At the heart of Christianity is God's desire for a people that displays His character. They do this through their obedience to His Word in their *relationships* with Him and with each other. Therefore He sent his Son to call out a people to follow Him. And part of our following the Son is calling still more to follow the Son. His Son therefore gave this last command before ascending to heaven: *go and make disciples* (Matthew 28:19). Therefore, the lives of these people, should be dedicated to *helping* others to follow Jesus.

DON'T BE CONFORMED

Unaware of the enormity of the cultural tsunami that has overrun the United States and Western Civilization since the sixties, many Christians and many local churches are *ill-equipped* to face the opposition that the new cosmology[15] is presenting. Certainly, most Christians have a sense that somethings are not right. I have spoken regularly to Christian churches, small groups and Bible students and hear them say that things are awful. How do we engage in this awful situation? It is imperative that we return to the *basics of the worldview* in order to respond to the present-day situations. Without such an analysis, believers may even *embrace* significant elements of what they do not realize is a very *unbiblical cosmology.[16]* And the trouble is, once you hear that stuff, it's in your knower. As I said earlier, many of our local churches are *ill-equipped* to engage this planned strategy of evil.

IF THE FOUNDATION ARE DESTROYED

---

[15] Cosmology is a branch of metaphysics that explores the fundamental nature of the universe. Most religions and cultures include some kind of cosmology to explain the nature of the universe. In modern astronomy the leading is still the Big Bang theory, which claims that the universe began with a huge explosion that sent matter and energy spreading in all directions. Accessed 3 Aug. 2024. Merriam-Webster.com dictionary, m/webster, https://www.meriam-webster,com/dictionary.

[16] Ibid.

In Psalm 11, King David grieves over the clashes of religious and cultural implosion, passionately expressing himself in a question that has often been quoted in churches throughout the past centuries. *"If the foundations are destroyed, what can the righteous do?"* (Psalm 11:3). When, like David, Christians see that *"the wicked bend the bow; they have fitted their arrow to the string to shoot in the dark at the upright in heart"* (Psa. 11:2), they are likely to follow the faulty advice offered by David's enemies: *"Flee like a bird to your mountain"* (Psa. 11:1). Some Christians have bought into this faulty advice and created closed communities stockpiled with supplies. And many of those who don't follow this path will still be tempted to disengage [frozen chosen].

No matter what it looks like, we must not give up or give in. Though the spiritual and moral foundations of this country (America) are shaken, though many have given *over to the "new worldview,"* we have enduring hope – for there is one *lasting* foundation. One sure place of refuge:

The Lord is in his holy temple,
the Lord's throne is in heaven,
his eyes see, his eyelids test the children of man,
The Lord tests the righteous,
but his soul hates the wicked and the one who loves
violence. ...
For the Lord is righteous.

He loves righteous deeds the upright shall behold his face (Psalms 11:4-5, 7).We know, with the eyes of faith, that clothed with his righteousness we shall "behold his face" (Psalms 11:7). Presently, what must the righteous do? Knowing that our Father is refining and testing us and that he loves "righteous deeds," even when the foundations are crumbling, we seek to display righteousness to the watching world. All the more, we can't quit or give in; even though that is the constant temptation when things get rough.

Today we face unprecedented opposition to the Christian faith. The response of believers is crucial for the survival of the gospel. This is a time not unparalleled with the beginning of church history – when religious paganism ruled the culture. Will the present church see the true nature of this situation and react in a way that will bring honor and glory to Christ and His gospel – as the early church did?

Conformity with the kind of world we have been describing above is the possible scenario. Conformity puts an immobilizing spirit of confusion overall. The apostles Peter (see 1 Peter 1:1, 14) and Paul (see Romans 12:2), both warned Christians against being conformed to this world. First century Christians lived under a regime that continually *tempted them to modify their beliefs and adapt their behavior to a culture that did not share their essential faith.* Christians throughout church history have been in similar social settings, in cultures and under governments that have absolutely no regard for Christian principles.

Christians, not just those in the United States, but the world over, are called by God in His Word to know the particular ideas that constitute the world's pattern of thinking and belief; in this way, we can both counter the Lie and make a statement of **the Truth** that understands and exposes **the lie** and offers the only true hope in the gospel. Spiritual ignorance or neglect of this commitment produces faith-destroying conformity and compromise.

FEARING THE CULTURE

Sadly, many Christians today often *conform* or *compromise* out of **fear.** We may fear verbal attacks, accusations of hate speech, or loss of friends, employment, or respect. Sometimes Christians receive threats of physical violence, and many are killed for their faith. The on-going campus unrest and reversals are reflections of **a new worldview.** Many of those people once known for unapologetic gospel preaching and open-air revivals are forced to take a low profile and others are forfeiting their biblical Christian worldview. How can Christians be an outpost for speaking gospel truth today on university campuses or any other venues when they are increasingly not allowed to speak at all?

THE PEACE OF GOD

Paul offers himself as an example, for his effort had been not only to teach Christianity – but to display it in his own life-living. Again, that his readers in past, present, and future generations may be sure of this protection when their one aim is to do what is right, and to be steadfast to the Christian faith.

Since it was not just another set of rules – but a new life altogether, it could be presented only through a living human being. He carefully defines:

1. How he had imparted the Christian knowledge.
2. He had done so first by instruction in the principles of the faith.
3. Then he handed down the tradition of how Jesus lived and died.
4. Then by counsels he had given to those who sought his guidance.
5. Then by his personal actions.

Therefore, the Philippians had seen for themselves, while he lived among them, how he followed the Christian teaching in spite of weakness, temptations, and persecutions. They must keep his example before them and act as he had done; and ***the God of peace will be with you. Amen.***

STUDY GUIDE: CHAPTER 12 SHAKE THE DUST OFF YOUR FEET

1. The apostles were to inquire, as they entered a village, for _____ of _____ _____.

2. The disciples would be welcomed by worthy folks; meaning worthy in spirit and worthy to receive the gospel of Christ. And through these the disciples could find others to tell the good news. Here we see the beginnings of the Christian missions.

3. Elsewhere the disciples might be _____, in such cases the apostles were to _____ the _____ off _____ _____.

4. Do you except your responsibility to help build and maintain a healthy local church?

5. Local churches exist to display God's glory to the nations.

6. They do this through their obedience to His Word in their relationships with Him and with each other.

7. If the foundations are destroyed, what can we do? We seek to display righteousness to the watching world.

SECTION FOUR
WINNING SOULS FOR CHRIST

CHAPTER THIRTEEN

Winning Tomorrow's World Today

"Have you considered my servant Job, that there is none like him on the earth, a blameless and upright man, who fears God and turns away from evil?" (Job 1:8 ESV)

Over the past several years increases in accidents and incidents on land, sea, and in the air seem to have become the norm. People are no longer shocked after hearing of a wheel falling from an airplane in mid-air, missing or loose bolts in death situations – unless of course they just happened to be on that particular plane. Even an amateur can make the call as to why this is happening. Not only aircrafts, trains, and the like, but even car seats for newborns, and millions of household items. Undoubtedly, money and other resources have a lot to do with this. During my military career I spent some years in tank-automotive maintenance.

For those years quality control was the key and highest priority. Even the work of the most excellent and experienced craftsmen, or repair personnel were inspected by quality assurance personnel before the equipment was released back to the unit.

I remember the GOOD HOUSEKEEPING SEAL (see Figure #1 & #2 next page) found on thousands of home products. While growing up a child, it was well-recognized and respected. That mark, with its distinctive logo, indicates that the product, process, or service has been rigorously tested to specific standards and complies with the requirements of those standards.

ORDER OUT OF CHAOS

A standard is defined as something *established* by an authority as a rule for measuring quality, weight, extent, value, or quality. Some synonyms for standard are *guideline, norm, yardstick, benchmark, gauge, measure, criterion, guide, model, pattern, example, rule, and law.* Standards are principles of conduct that support an established rule.

Generally, a standard allows some acceptable variation or deviation, although the range is typically quite narrow, allowing a standard's quality qualifications to be met if the final result is within the range. It also identifies potentially dangerous "discrepancies" that must be reworked or discarded.

FIGURES #1 and #2 BELOW

Good Housekeeping, 2010 | Flickr - Photo Sharing! by Unknown Author is licensed under CC BY-NC

Good Housekeeping, 2010 | Flickr - Photo Sharing! by Unknown Author is licensed under CC BY-NC

FIGURE #2

Daily, we encounter many products, processes, and services resulting from human ingenuity. We take it for granted that they will function, yet we seldom consider the standards that help ensure that functioning. Standards bring *order* and *safety* to our lives, and most people would agree that they are essential.

DOES GOD HAVE STANDARDS?

When we look at His creation and see that He does. All around us we see order, beauty, and purpose. When God builds something, He does a perfect job. He works to a high standard. God is our Creator and He alone has complete technical knowledge and experience as to how we are made and how *best* we can function. Different than animals or plants – He has made us *in His image and likeness.* And because we reflect His image and likeness, He expects us to live our lives to a higher standard, which we find reflected in His Word.

In our text, Job 1:8, God says to Satan, *"Have you considered My servant Job, that there is none like him on the earth, a blameless and upright man, one who fears God and shuns evil?"* [Is this how God would describe us?]. Are we doing *evil,* or are we doing what is *right in His eyes?* God sets the standards; and the only judgment that ultimately matters is His. How do we measure up to the higher standard that God has given us? That standard is essential.

God sets the standards, and the only judgment that ultimately matters is His!

UNBIASED PRINCIPLES

Unbiased principles based on the eternal truths of God's Word that *determine* right and wrong behavior *do exist but* are usually overlooked. The Holy Bible contains standards of conduct that, *when obeyed,* bring great benefits. If these standards are not followed, the results are disastrous. Sadly, these timeless principles are being taught and practiced less and less in each new generation.

Problems resulting from this departure from established moral standards have proven to be devastating. The weakening of biblical marriage and the family structures – a man at the head, his wife by his side, with their children following their lead – carries with it too many negative connotations on today's society to cover them all here. Miseducation has terribly undermined *basic skills* by teaching critical theory rather than the basic knowledge required to excel in life today.

Cultural degeneration has led to increasingly more vicious and violent crimes, predatory sexual practices and human trafficking, gender confusion, drug addiction, fraudulent business dealings, and racial tensions. Even as disruption and clamor rise amongst the citizenry for solutions, governments are unable or unwilling to make helpful and meaningful changes to eradicate these problems.

In His eternal Word, the Bible, God has listed the benefits of obedience to His standards of conduct and the terrible problems that would occur if His ways were despised or ignored. Leviticus 26 and Deuteronomy 28 make it quite clear that if a person or nation desires peace and prosperity, obedience to God is not optional! "Do you know that the unrighteous will not inherit the kingdom of God? Do not be deceived: neither the sexually immoral, nor idolater, nor adulterers, nor people who practice homosexuality, nor thieves, nor the greedy, nor drunkards, no revilers, nor swindlers will inherit the kingdom of God." (1 Corinthians 6:9-10 ESV)

Many other passages of Scripture plainly prohibit licentious sexual practices. But this is not merely Old Testament instruction. The Apostle Paul described in detail the cause and consequences of such behavior (study prayerfully Romans 1:18-32).

Paul went on to explain that these unrighteous acts would be forgiven after sincere repentance and the acceptance of Christ's sacrifice for the remission of sin. The Apostle Peter put it this way:

> "Repent and let everyone of you be baptized in the name of Jesus for the remission of sins; and you shall receive the Holy Spirit. For the promise is to you and to your children, and to all who are afar off, as many as the Lord our God will call to Himself." (Acts 2:38-39 ESV)

YOU ARE SAVED

Browsing through the employment section of the newspaper's classified ads, you will usually find a variety of entries to meet almost any need. However, here is one you *will not see*, but any one of us might have placed at some point in our lives:

"WANTED: MASTER CRAFTSMAN NEEDED TO REMODEL DAMAGED LIFE. Current life has been damaged beyond normal repairs due to original sin. The owner has tried a variety of ways to correct the problem but has failed every time. The qualified applicant must have the following:

1. Must have own tools.
2. Must be willing to work.
3. Must have impeccable references.
4. Must have a previous successful track record with similar restorations.
5. Must be willing to work for nothing.
   The owner cannot pay anything.

The owner is willing to work for the Master Craftsman upon successful completion of his remodeled life.

There is an immediate need to fill this position.
Call 1-800-REMODEL for an appointment."[17]

This classified ad closely resembles the cry of every Christian before salvation. Our damaged lives are beyond human repair – and *all* of our efforts to correct the problem have failed. We thank and praise the Master Craftsman, our Lord Jesus, was qualified to answer the ad:

• He had all the tools needed to save us.
• He was willing to provide the work needed to save us.
• He was referred to us by His Father.
• His track record is all of the other saints that have gone before us.
• Finally, He would not accept payment for our salvation.

You are saved by God alone. This fact cannot be overemphasized! You are saved by God's *grace*. Grace means the unmerited favor and kindness of God. However, there is a *uniqueness* about God's favor and kindness. His favor and kindness are given despite the fact that it is

---

[17] Illustration adapted from the TEACHER'S OUTLINE & BIBLE, Leadership Ministries Worldwide (1996)

undeserved and *unmerited*. God has done this among us, human beings despite their ...

- cursing Him,
- rejecting Him,
- rebelling against Him,
- denial of Him,
- neglect of Him,
- hostility toward Him,
- half-hearted commitment to Him,
- worship of religion rather than worship of Him,
- false worship
- idolatrous worship
- trespasses and sins

Grace is giving, but it is giving to people who do not deserve it. It is so easy today to forget the gift that God has given, Jesus Christ. God has given His Son, Jesus Christ, to save people. Understand, God did not have to do that. Humanity deserved to be wiped from the face of the earth, but this is truly God's grace.

When Jesus Christ hung on the cross, He was taking our sins upon Himself and bearing the punishment for our sins. Christ took our penalty and condemnation upon Himself. He died for us – in our place as our substitute. The Scripture says,

> *"But God commended His love toward us, in that, while we were yet sinners, Christ died for us."* (Romans 5:8)

YOU ARE SAVED THROUGH FAITH

What does this mean? It means this: Jesus Christ died for us. He bore our sin and punishment upon the cross. Believing that Jesus really died for us. God takes our faith and counts it as the death of Jesus Christ for us. That is, when we honor God's dear Son by believing in Him so much that we give all that we are and all that we have to Him, God takes the death of Christ and applies it to us. Our faith causes God to look upon us as having been *in* Christ when He died. It is our faith that causes God to credit us with salvation. Jesus Christ is God's gift to us. Salvation through

Christ has been wrapped up as a gift and God hands it over to us. A gift is not ours until we believe it is ours and we take and receive it.

YOU CAN'T SAVE YOURSELF

As I stated earlier, you are saved through faith in Jesus Christ. God is perfect, and to live in His presence, a person must be perfect. This is the great problem of man. Humans are not perfect; therefore he or she can never live in God's presence – not in and of themself. Even if a person could be good enough and do enough good to become perfect (he cannot, but even if he could) he would not be acceptable to God. Why?

Because he has already transgressed and become imperfect. He already stands imperfect, if he is ever to be perfected and have his past wiped clean – it certainly won't be his doing. He cannot save himself. Salvation is of God, not of man.

> *"For by grace are ye saved through faith; and that not of yourselves: it is the gift of God: not of works, lest any man should boast."* (Ephesians 2:8-9 KJV)

YOU ARE GOD'S WORKMANSHIP

We are God's workmanship – **created in Christ Jesus.** The gospel believer experiences two creations, both a natural birth and a spiritual birth. The spiritual birth holds the emphasis in this verse. When a person believes in Jesus Christ, God creates him or her in Christ, meaning:

1. God, the Holy Spirit *quickens the spirit* of the believer and makes his or her spirit alive (regeneration). Whereas the believer's spirit was dead, to God, the Holy Spirit creates it new and makes it alive unto God. (see Eph. 2:1, 5).

2. God causes the believer to be *born again spiritually.* (see John 3:3, 5-6).

3. God actually places His *divine nature* into the heart of the believer. (see John 3:3, 5-6).

4. God actually makes *a new creature* of the believer. (see 2 Corinthians 5:17).

5. God actually creates a *new person* out of the believer. (see Ephesians 4:24).

6. God renews the believer by the Holy Spirit. (see Titus 3:5).

WE ARE CREATED TO DO GOOD WORKS

God saves man for good works *not* by good works. He fashions man and creates a masterpiece, a work of art. The believer just shows that he is God's workmanship by the life he or she lives and displays. Works are an evidence of salvation. Those who walk in trespasses and sins indicate that they are not God's workmanship no matter what they profess (see Ephesians 2:1-2). God's people give ample evidence of *the power of a new life* operating within them.

God has ordained us to walk in good works. Doing good works is not an option for the believer; it is the very nature of the believer. If a person has been created in Christ. If God has truly worked in that person, then they do good works. His or her very nature dictates that. He cannot do otherwise. He is not perfect, and he fails; but he keeps coming back to God and falling upon his knees, believing and asking forgiveness, and getting back up and going forth once again to do the good he or she can. As stated, it is their nature. He or she is a new creature created to do good works. So, they do them Just like a tree, he or she bears the fruit of their nature.

> *"Let your light so shine before men, that they may see your good works, and glorify your Father which is in heaven."* (Matthew 5:16)

Jay Leach

STUDY GUIDE: CHAPTER 13 WINNING TOMORROW'S WORLD TODAY

1. A standard is defined established by an authority as a rule for measuring quality, weight, extent, value, or quality.

2. Grace is _____, but it is _____ to people who do not _____ it.

3. When Jesus Christ hung on the cross, He was taking our sins upon Himself and bearing the _____ for our _____.

4. Our faith causes God to look upon us as having been ____ _____ _____ _____ _____.

5. God actually places His _____ _____ into the heart of the believer.

6. God actually _____ a new _____, out of the _____.

7. God has _____ us to walk in _____ _____.

CHAPTER FOURTEEN

A Mature Person In Christ

"Now unto Him that is able to do exceedingly abundantly
above all that we ask or think, according to the power
that worketh in us." (Ephesians 3:20 KJV)

I have never met a person who took a test without wanting to know what to study. Nor have I met a soldier who was willing to go into battle without his weapon. But I have met Christians who are perfectly willing to live their lives without God's power. Why? Possibly, due to ignorance of how to tap into God's vast arsenal of power. While others may have heard of God's power; they would rather supply their *own source* of strength.

If we Christians fail to connect into God's power, the results spill out in how we live: The fruit within us spoils. We take our relationship with God and turn it into just another religion. Without the power of God, Christianity becomes an empty form. As Paul told Timothy, *"Having a form of godliness, but denying the power."* (2 Timothy 3:5)

In the Book of Ephesians, the apostle Paul balances doctrine and duty. First Paul reminds Christians in Christ what God has done for us; then he tells us what do for Him; in response to His mercies. Christian living to maturity is based on Christian learning. The believer who does *not* know his or her wealth in Christ will never be able to walk for Christ. Our conduct depends on our calling.

Christian living to maturity is based on Christian learning.

Too many Christians live in Ephesians 1-3 and study the doctrines but fail to move into chapters 4-6 and practice the duties.

BLESSINGS FROM THE FATHER (1:1-6)

- **He chose us** not in ourselves; but He chose us in Christ, by grace (see verses 3-4; 1 Corinthians 1:26-29; 2 Thessalonians 2:13-14; and John 6:37).
- **He has adopted us.** Adoption in the New Testament refers to the official act of a father who bestows the status of full adulthood on a son of minor status (v. 5).
- **He has accepted us.** In ourselves, we are not acceptable to God, but in Christ, we are "made accepted" (v. 6).

BLESSINGS FROM THE SON (1:7-12)

- **He has redeemed us (7a).** By giving His life on the cross, Christ purchased us from the slavery of sin. We have been redeemed. He has delivered us from the penalty and power of sin; we shall have a future redemption (v. 14) when Christ delivers us from the presence of sin at His return.
- **He has revealed (7b).** The word "forgive" literally means "to send away." Sin is a terrible burden that is sent away when a sinner turns to Christ. Christ carried the burden on the cross (see 1 Peter 2:24; also see Lev. 16:20-2).
- **He has made us an inheritance (vv. 11-12).** God has not only given us an inheritance in Christ (see 1 Peter 3-4), but He made us an inheritance for Christ. The church is His body, temple, and bride; we shall someday share His glory.

BLESSINGS FROM THE HOLY SPIRIT (1:13- 14)

- **He has sealed us (v. 13).** This important verse outlines the way of salvation. The sinner hears the Word of Truth, trusts in Christ, receives the Holy Spirit, and is sealed forever. This sealing means God owns us and will keep us. God's seal is unbreakable.

He has given us an earnest (v. 14).

"Ernest money" in business means money given as a down pay for a purchased possession. God has given us His Spirit as the "down payment" to assure us that we will experience total redemption and receive God's promised blessings in glory.

At the end of each section, notice Paul tells why the Father, Son, and the Holy Spirit have given us these blessings: "To the praise of His glory" (vv. 6, 12, 14b). Salvation is by God's grace and for His glory! God does not have to save anybody; when He does save the sinner. He does so for His own glory.

PRAYER FOR UNDERSTANDING (1:15-23)

We find two prayers in Ephesians 1, they are: *#1 Enlightenment: "that you might know,"* (1:15-23) *and #2 Enablement: "that you might be,"*(3:13-21). The first prayer is for our *enlightenment,* and the second is for *enablement.* Paul prays first that we might *know* what Christ has done for us; then he prays that we might *live* up to these wonderful blessings and put them to work in our daily lives. Notice his requests:

1. *That God may give you spiritual understanding (vv. 17-18a).*

   Spiritual truth must be spiritually discerned (1 Corinthians 2:9-16), and this understanding can come only from the Spirit. Remember, He wrote the Word and He alone can teach us what it says.

2. *That you might know the hope of His calling (v. 18b).*

Because God chose us in Christ before the foundation of the world, we have a blessed hope for all eternity that depends not on our goodness, but on His grace.

3. *That you might know the riches of His inheritance (v. 18c).*

We only have an inheritance in Christ, but we are an inheritance to Christ (see v. 11). Christians **mature** in the Lord when they learn how much they mean to Christ – then start living to bring joy to His heart.

4. *That you might know His power (vv. 19-23).*

The very power that raised Jesus from the dead is available for our daily lives! Christ has already won the victory over sin, death, the world and Satan. God's people do not fight for victory but from victory!

However, all these blessings are only for those who meet the conditions set forth in vv. 1-2. Note that Paul writes to living saints – people who have put their faith in Christ. These saints (set apart ones) have *experienced* God's grace and now enjoy God's peace. The Bible does not teach that any church can makes people saints. Only God can make a sinner a saint. And the sinner must become a saint while he or she is still alive, for after death is the judgment (see Hebrews 9:27).

As we close this chapter, it would be helpful to note Paul's "spiritual postures," for they give us the secret of God's blessing. Paul is seated with Christ (2:6), built upon Christ (2:20), and is bowing His knees to the Father (3:14). This makes it possible for him to walk (4:1), grow up (4:15), and stand against Satan (6:14). Our spiritual position in Christ makes possible our victorious walk on earth.

STUDY GUIDE: CHAPTER 14
A MATURE PERSON IN CHRIST

1. Why are so many Christians willing to live their lives without
   _____ _____?

2. Without the power of God, Christianity becomes an
   _____ _____.

3. The believer who does not know his or her _____ in Christ
   will never be able to walk for Christ.

4. Salvation is by God's _____ and for His _____.

5. We find two prayers in Ephesians 1, they are #1 *"that you might
   know,"* (1:15-23) and #2 *"that you might be,"* (3:13-21).

6. The very power that raised Jesus from the dead is available for our
   _____ _____.

7. Christ has already won the victory over sin, death, the world, and
   Satan. God's people do not fight for victory, but from victory.

CHAPTER FIFTEEN

Our Walk With Christ

*"For this reason I bow my knees before the **Father**, from whom every family in heaven and on earth is named, that according to the riches of His glory he may grant you to be strengthened with **power** through his Spirit in your inner being, so that Christ may dwell in your hearts through **faith** – that you, being rooted and grounded **in love**, may have strength to comprehend with all the **saints** what is the breadth and length and height, an depth, and to **know** the love of Christ that surpasses knowledge, that you may be filled with all the fullness of God."* (Ephesians 3:14-19 ESV)

The Christian life is compared to a walk because it starts with *one step of faith*, involves progress, and demands balance and strength. If we never learn to walk, we will never be able to run (see Hebrews 12:1-2) or stand in battle (see Ephesians 6:11).

WALK IN UNITY (4:1-16)

We have been called to one body; therefore, as we seek to walk in unity, we are walking worthy of the calling (vocation) we have from God. Paul has described this high calling in chapters 1-3; now he pleads with us to live up to these blessings. We do not live for Christ just to get more stuff as is implied by many on social media today; but we live for Christ because He has already done so much for us! Please note that Paul does not tell us to make up or manufacture unity, but to maintain the unity *already existing* in the body. See John 17:20-23,

> *"I do not ask for these only, but also for those who will believe in me through their word, that they may all be one, just as you, Father, are in me, and I in you, that they also may be in us, so that the world may believe that you have sent me. The glory that you have given me I have given to them, that they may be one even as we are one, I in them and you in me, that they may become perfectly one, so that the world may know that you sent me and loved them even as you have loved me. (ESV)*

It's important to note that the grounds for this unity and center in this listing is **"one Lord."** (see Ephesians 4:4-6). In this opening section of the letter's second half Paul is appealing for *every* believer to fully understand the process needed to attain unity and spiritual maturity in the church. The process includes both *being equipped* (v. 12) and participating in the ministry (vv. 15-16). Unity is the responsibility of each believer and is to be pursued earnestly. The fact that there is **"one body"** does not negate the importance of the local bodies of believers (local churches). Here Paul is dealing with spiritual truths pertaining to the whole program of God. When we read his other epistles (as Corinthians, and the letters to Timothy and Titus); we see the practicality of these truths.

Remember, the major emphasis in the New Testament pertains to the local assembly; however, the administration of the local assembly (church) must be based on what Paul teaches about the "one body."

SPIRITUAL GIFTS FOR UNITY

The gifts for unity in the church are given in (vv. 7-11). When Christ ascended, on high He led a host of captives, and He gave gifts to men through the coming of the Holy Spirit. And He gave some apostles, the prophets, the evangelists, the shepherds, and teachers, *to equip the saints for the work of ministry, for the building up the body of Christ until we all attain to the unity of the faith and of the knowledge of the Son of God, to mature manhood, to the measure of the stature of the fulness of Christ.*

The five ministry offices listed here are gifts that Christ gave for the *nurture* and *maturing* and *equipping* (that is, to mend, prepare, and enable to function) *of His church*, not for hierarchical control or ecclesiastical competition. Beyond the distinct role filled by the original founding apostles. The pastor and teacher are to "make disciples" by nourishing the saints through the Spirit and the Word of God, and equipping (a making fit, preparing, training, perfecting, making fully qualified for service), these saints (disciples) in turn, perform the work of the ministry. Emphasis is mine.

As each saint grows to spiritual maturity and win others, the entire body being built up by the *mutual efforts* of all the members to grow in Christ. Each saint (disciple) shares in the growth of the local church. Unfortunately, there are some Christians who are still babes in Christ (see v.v. 14, also see 2 Corinthians 11:14-15) are easily swayed by Satan's lies. The church is edified (built up) through the Spirit and the Word (see Acts 20:32 and 1 Corinthians 14:4).

Churches are not built up and strengthened through fads and man-made programs, entertainment, recreations, and fund drives. The church is a body and must have spiritual food; that food is the Word of God. When the body of Christ is completed, He will return and take His body home to glory (1:22-23).

WALK IN PURITY (Ephesians 4:17-32)

In the first part of this chapter Paul described the believer's relationship to the church; here He deals with the believer's relationship to the world. Although we are "in Christ" and a part of the body; we are also in the world, where there is temptation and defilement. We cannot leave the world because we have a responsibility to witness and win it; but we must walk in purity and not allow the world to defile.

Paul begins with the negative: do not walk the way the unsaved walk. He gives five traits of a worldly walk summed up in the word *futility, GK word (cease to care)*

1. Darkened understanding
2. Alienation from God
3. Ignorance of God's way
4. Hardened hearts
5. An unfeeling state

Today we might summarize their plight by saying they were walking in the wrong direction because they did not know the truth and had never received the life. Only the Christ of John 14:6 could meet their spiritual needs. The Christian life must be radically different from the old life. Paul expected the Ephesians to experience changes and he gave three admonitions:

1. "put off" (vv. 22-23)
2. "put on" (v. 24)
3. "put away" (vv. 25)

As presented in earlier chapters, Romans 6 teaches us that the old self has been crucified and buried, and that, as we reckon this to be true, we "put off" the old man. God has done His part; it remains for us to believe what He has said and "change clothes."

The instruction Jesus gave concerning Lazarus applies to each believer: "Loose him – take off the grave clothes – and let him go!" But it is not complete simply to die to the old life; *there must also be a resurrection and the manifestation of the new life.* We put off the "grave clothes" of the old life and put on the "grace clothes" of the "new life." We are part of God's new creation (v. 24 and 2:10) and therefore we walk in newness of life (see Romans 6:4). We must "put away" (once-for-all) certain sins, and he names them:

1. Put away all lying (v. 25)
2. Be angry and do not sin (v. 26)

3. Don't give place to the devil (v. 27)
4. Let him who stole steal no longer (v. 28)
5. Let no corrupt word proceed out of your mouth (v. 29)
6. Do not grieve the Holy Spirit of God (v. 30)
7. Let all bitterness, wrath, anger, clamor, and evil speaking be put away from you, with all malice (v. 31)
8. And be kind to one another, tender-hearted, forgiving one another, even as God in Christ forgave you (v. 32)

This is important: Jesus taught the duty of *forgiving* and showed it to be fundamental to having one's own prayers for forgiveness answered (study carefully, Matthew 6:14, 15, 18:21-35).

WALK IN LOVE (Eph. 5:1-6)

Paul admonishes, that we walk in love as Christ has loved us and gave Himself for us, an offering and a sacrifice to God for a sweet-smelling aroma (see 5:1-2). Because of the great love God has for us, He has cleansed us by the blood of Jesus, making us holy by His grace and mercy. We cannot earn His forgiveness or become holy through our own works.

IT IS BY GRACE THROUGH FAITH IN JESUS THAT WE ARE MADE RIGHTEOUS.

It is by grace through faith in Jesus that we are made righteous. However, God has created us to do good works, things He prepared in advance for us to do. Do the good things God gives you to do but know that you are holy by His grace.

Knowing that God raised you up out of death into life and positioned you securely in Christ. Compare vv. 5-6 with Galatians 5:21 and 1 Corinthians 6:9-10. False teachers are everywhere today, and many people are being led astray by them with the **lie:** They may say that you can be a Christian and live in habitual, deliberate sin; but Paul calls these teachers *"empty [vain] words.*

WALK AS CHILDREN OF LIGHT (Ephesians 5:7-14)

We were once *partakers* with the "children of disobedience" (2:1-3); now we are children of God, and we ought to walk in the light (vv. 7-8). The word translated "partakers" in v. 7, implies having in common; and often translated "fellowship" or Partnership." Christians are partakers of:

1. the divine nature, (2 Peter 1:4)
2. God's promises, (Ephesians 3:6)
3. Christ's sufferings, (1 Peter 4:13)
4. Holiness, (Hebrews 12:10)
5. the heavenly calling, (Hebrews3:1)
6. God's glory (1 Peter 5:1)

Since we have this beautiful partnership with God, how could we become partners with that which belongs to sin and darkness? "What communication has light with darkness?" asks 2 Corinthians 6:14 NKJV. We are children of light and ought to walk in the light. The light cannot compromise with the darkness; it can only expose it. (see John 3:19-21 and 1 John 1:5-10).

WALK CAREFULLY (5:15-17)

The word "circumspectly" (v. 15) carries the idea of looking around carefully so as not to stumble. It means walking intelligently and not in ignorance. How foolish it is to stumble along through life and never seek to know the will of the Lord. Instead of walking "circumspectly," they miss the mark, miss the road, and end up stuck on some side road going nowhere. God desires that we be wise and understand His will for our lives.

As we obey His will, we *redeem* the time (v. 16) and do not waste time, energy, money, and talent in that which is apart from His will. Lost opportunities may never be regained; they are gone forever. Each of us needs to take a moment to think through where we waste so much time and correct it. More than ever, we need to give ourselves to make a significant contribution to our work and society, to our church and community, to living righteously, and godly, *to witnessing and helping a world who are discouraged and lonely, hungry and cold, hurting and suffering, needy and helpless – all lost in sin – all without the knowledge of Christ and of eternal life.* The call of the hour is to redeem the time! (study 2 Cor. 10:5; Ps. 90:12).

In a typical 24-hour day, how much of your time is spent doing these activities:

Activity   **# of Hours**
Prayer/worship:
Work:
Family Time:
TV/Videos:
Recreation:
Sleep:
Which area needs to be adjusted first?
Why is it important to redeem the time?
What kind of things can you do to be a better steward of your time?[18]

WALK IN HARMONY (5:18-6:9)

The secret of harmony in the home and on the job is the fullness of the Spirit. The unity of the church and the harmony of the home both depend on the Spirit (4:3; 5:18).

IT IS POWER FROM WITHIN, NOT PRESSURE FROM WITHOUT, THAT HOLDS THE CHURCH AND THE HOME TOGETHER.

Notice the evidence of a Spirit-filled life: joy (v. 19), gratitude (v. 20), obedience (v. 21). Compare Colossians 3:15-17 and you will see that when Christians are filled with the Word of God, they will have the same characteristics. In other words, to be filled with the Spirit of God means to be controlled by the Word of God. The marks of a Spirit-filled Christian are character and fruit of the Spirit (see Galatians 5:22, 23).

---

[18] Adapted from: The Teacher's Outline & Study Bible by Alpha-Omega Ministries, Inc, (1996) 168

TO BE FILLED WITH THE SPIRIT OF GOD MEANS TO BE CONTROLLED BY THE WORD OF GOD!

The *principle* of headship is what helps bring harmony to the home. "As unto Christ" is the motive. Wives are to submit to their husbands as unto Christ; husbands are to love their wives as Christ loves the church; and children are to obey as unto the Lord. Family members in the right relationship with the Lord will be right with each other.

Methods change but principles remain the same!

The church is pictured as the bride of Christ. It is quite interesting to compare the church to the first bride in the Bible. Eve (Genesis 2:18-25). God took her from the side of Adam – and Christ's side was pierced for us on the cross. She was formed while Adam was asleep, and Christ experienced the sleep of death to create the church. Eve shared Adam's nature, and the church partakes of Christ's nature (vv. 30-31). Eve was the recipient of Adam's love and care, and Christ loves the church and cares for it. Adam was willing to become a sinner because of his love for his wife (see 1 Timothy 2:11-15), and Christ was willingly made sin because of His love for the church. Eve was formed and brought to Adam before sin entered humanity; the church was in the mind and heart of God before the foundation of the world. Prayerfully study, Romans 7:4 and 2 Corinthians 11:2 for the application of this truth of marriage to the individual believer and the local church.

What is Christ's present ministry to the church? He is sanctifying and cleansing the church through the Word of God, and He does this by the work of the Holy Spirit in the believer. Paul was willing to suffer death for Jesus' sake and for the sake of the churches. The experiences that brought death to Paul *meant* life for the believers as he suffered to bring the Word of God to them. He points to his scars as the credentials of his ministry. (see 4:11-16). The Word is not only water that cleanses the church, but it is also food that nourishes the church (v. 29).

THE WORD OF GOD IS THE SPIRITUAL FOOD FOR THE *NEW NATURE OF THE BELIEVER.*

GUIDELINES FOR THE FAMILY IN THE LORD (Ephesians 6:1-4)

In 6:1-4, the guidelines are for the family in the Lord and are not necessarily expected to work outside of the believing. Children are to obey their parents in the Lord for several reasons:

1. It is right
2. It is commanded
3. It brings blessings

The father who honors the Lord will not normally have trouble winning the love and respect of his children or the sincere love of his wife. Paul also warns fathers in (v. 4) to refrain from provoking their children with undue demands. The Golden Rule applies to the home, and children must be treated like people and not things. Fathers are to discipline children (nurture) and counsel them (admonition) in the Lord.

DIM PROSPECTS

Today's generation consists of adult children of parents who were themselves young adults in the sixties. You might continue to believe and expect to see the positive effects of a liberated new humanity on family structure and morals, but don't count on it. One commentator observed, "The sexual revolution that began in the 1960s has borne its fruit:

- More violence
- Abortions
- Pornography
- Suicides
- Absentee fathers
- Single-parent homes

- Overwhelmed mothers
- Children who roam the streets
- Sex before marriage
- Disobedient children
- Children absent from churches
- Poverty
- Mental problems
- Murder and mayhem (drive-by and otherwise)
- Wides-spread violence
- Majority no longer have any connection with the church
- Widespread STDs, AIDS, teen pregnancies, and the list goes on!

AMERICA THE BEAUTIFUL

Before the sixties revolution America was the epicenter of Christianity in the 20th Century world, the nation sent countless missionaries to mission fields around the world. Christianity was everywhere, as evidenced by the uncountable number of radio and television stations, Christian schools, and Bible colleges, Christian publishers, and church buildings in every direction. It was common to hear the saints speak of the "prayer covering" over this country.

My motivation for writing this book is out of my concern in helping to explain the origin and nature of this transformation and its effects within contemporary western culture in such a short time.

DEVISTATED TRANSFORMATION

The rules have changed – the western culture has tumbled off the track. In our lifetime, the "prayer canopy" of a Chrisitan civilization for the most part has been taken down, replaced by a *new* overarching structure of *spiritual beliefs* and *practices*. Many of the plausible structures that *gave meaning* and *significance* under Christian influence in the United States and the West are unrecognizable today, take a look:

- Morality has been relativized by various (and often contradictory) personal or social convictions.
- Honesty means being true to one's *inner* commitments and desires more than to external expectations or *objective facts*.

- Acceptable models of sexuality, marriage and the family *allow* various combinations of persons and genders.
- Marriage is often functionally indistinguishable from mutually convenient cohabitation.
- Motherhood is celebrated in the same breath as abortion on demand.

The meaning and context of spirituality and religion have undergone a drastic paradigm shift no less fundamental. The very idea of a God now allows for polytheism (many gods) or pantheism (a god identical with the universe). The average millennial or Gen Z in the United States no longer defines *a vital spiritual life* as knowledge of and communion with the infinite-yet-personal Creator God of the heaven and earth who is revealed in the Bible.

SPIRITUALITY HAS BECOME A DO-IT-YOURSELF (YOUR THING) THAT BLENDS ANCIENT EASTERN PRACTICES WITH MODERN CONSUMER SENSIBILITIES.

For many people religion is merely an admission that we are all grasping for being spiritual but not religious? I'm not trying to make a case to return to the culture of the Fifties. In that era, people were just as sinful and had just as many problems, such as institutional racism and sexism. Nevertheless, that culture, with changeable degrees of success and consistency, existed under the "prayer covering" of a *basic* Christian worldview, so that fundamental ideas about God, morality, sexuality, marriage and the family, motherhood, spirituality, and religion – were understood from a Christian perspective, consciously or unconsciously. People missed the mark, but everyone was assuming generally the same marks. I have watched this "devastated transformation" occur in the time of one generation. I've observed it on several continents and preached, lectured and written about it. It is my prayer that by God's grace, this reflection and research will allow me some success in analyzing what *is happening* now and what Christians, who are called to be *salt* and *light,* can do about it. Certainly, the goal is not to recover a 20th Century

Western culture, but to preach the gospel clearly in our own time and bless the culture with God-honoring living. The changed culture in which we live is the only one young readers have known. Current generations may accept contemporary *beliefs* and *lifestyle choices* without realizing just how abnormal they were just a few years ago. Wisdom from the surrounding culture, whose assumptions and values are often un-Christian. While we should desire to understand our culture in order to bear witness to Jesus in it, we must *avoid conforming* to its expectations just to receive its affirmation.

Most importantly, as the church, we must *call all cultures – and ourselves* in every generation to the rule that judges all other rules – the *rule of faith*, the law of true freedom, the Word of God.

WE WILL NOT ADJUST THE BIBLE TO THE AGE
BUT
WE WILL ADJUST THE AGE TO THE BIBLE!
PASTOR CHARLES SPURGEON

---

2 Corinthians 4:18 is a paradox to the unbeliever, but a precious truth to the Christian. We live by faith, not by sight. It is faith that enables the Christian to see things that cannot be seen (Hebrews 11:1-3); this faith comes from the Word of God (Romans 10:17). The things that the world lives and dies for are temporal, passing; the things of the Lord last forever. The world thinks we are crazy because we dare to believe God's Word and live according to His will. We pass up the "things" that men covet because our hearts are set on higher values.

It is imperative that we have a sincere Christian life and ministry. Our motives must be pure. Our methods must be scriptural. We must be true to the Word of God. Paul had this kind of ministry and so should we!

STUDY GUIDE: CHAPTER 15
OUR WALK WITH CHRIST

1. The major emphasis of the New Testament pertains to the
   _____ _____.

2. As each saint grows to spiritual maturity and win others to
   Christ, the entire body being built up by the _____
   _____ of all the members to grow in Christ.

3. The church is a body and must have spiritual food, that food is the
   _____ of _____.

4. Although we are "in Christ" and a part of the body; we are also in the
   world, where there is _____ and _____.

5. Roman 6 teaches us that the old self has been crucified and buried,
   and that, as we _____ this to be true, we _____ _____
   the old man.

6. The instruction Jesus gave concerning Lazarus applies to each
   believer: "Loose him – take off the grave clothes – and let him
   go. But it is not complete simply to die to the old life; there must
   also be a _____ and the _____ of the
   _____ _____.

7. We cannot earn God's _____ or become
   _____ through our own works.

CHAPTER SIXTEEN

Walking In Victory

"Finally my brethren, be strong in the Lord and in the power of His might. Put on the whole armor of God, that you may be able to stand against the wiles of the devil.' For we do not wrestle against flesh and blood, but against principalities, against powers, against the rulers of the darkness of the age, against spiritual hosts of wickedness in the heavenly places." (Ephesians 6:11-12 NKJV)

In this chapter (vv. 10-24) Paul tells us how to walk-in victory. It is a terrible thing when believers don't know the provisions God has made for victory over Satan. Christ has *completely overcome* Satan and his hosts (see Col. 2:13-15 and Eph. 1:19-23), and His victory is ours by faith.

SATAN, THE ENEMY (6:10-12)

Satan is a very formidable enemy, so Paul exhorts us to be strong. Paul knows that the flesh is weak (see Mark 14:38) and that we can overcome only in Christ's power. He commands us to be strong in v. 10, then he tells us to stand in v. 11. How do we get the strength to stand?

By realizing that we are seated in the heavenlies far above all of Satan's principalities, and powers (see 1:19-23), and that the very power of God is available to us through the indwelling Spirit (3:14-21). So, we must sit before we can walk, and we must walk before we can stand. We must understand our spiritual position before we can have *spiritual power.*

Many Bible students believe that Satan was the anointed cherub whom God placed in charge of the newly created earth (see Ezekiel 28:11-19). Through pride, he fell (see Isaiah 14:9) and took with him a host of angelic beings who now make up his army of principalities and powers. Satan has access to heaven (see Job 1-3), but one day will be cast from heaven (Revelation 12:9). He is a deceiver (2 Corinthians 11:3) and the destroyer (Revelation 9:11). The Apostle Peter warns that Satan goes about as a snake and a lion (1 Peter 5:8-9).

Christians need to realize that we do not fight against flesh and blood but against the **"spirit who now works in the sons of disobedience"** (see Ephesians 2:2 NKJV). Just as the Spirit of God works in the believer – Satan and his demons work in the lives of unbelievers. It is very foolish to fight flesh and blood when the real enemy is merely using that flesh and blood to block the Lord's work. This is the mistake Peter made in the Garden of Gethsemane when he tried to overcome the devil with

The sword (see Matthew 26:51). Moses made the same mistake when he killed the Egyptian (Acts 7:23-29). The only way to fight spiritual enemies is with the Word of God and prayer.

We must be on guard and beware of the wiles of the devil (Ephesians 6:11) which means his strategies and devices (2 Corinthians 2:11) and snares (1 Timothy 3:7). He is the ruler of darkness and uses darkness (ignorance and lies) to further his cause (2 Corinthians 4:1-6; Luke 22:53).

THE ARMOR WE WEAR (6:13-17)

The Scripture warns us as Christians to not *"give place to the devil"* (4:27), that is, don't leave any area unprotected, so that Satan can get a foothold. The armor Paul describes is for our protection; and the sword (God's Word) is our offensive and defense weapon in battle. Each part of the armor tells us what the believers must have if they are to be protected against Satan:

Truth – Satan is a liar, but the Christian who knows the *truth* will not be deceived.

Righteousness – Here the consistent daily walk of the Christian is in full view. Satan is the accuser (see Rev. 12:10), but the Christian who walks in the light will thwart Satan's opportunity to attack. We stand in the *imputed righteousness* of Christ, and we walk in the *imparted righteousness* of the Holy Spirit.

Peace – Satan is a destroyer, and a divider. What he can't destroy, he attempts to contaminate. When the believer walks in the way of *peace,* the Gospel way, then Satan cannot reach him or her. The believers' feet should be clean (see John 13), beautiful (Romans 10:15), and shod with the Gospel. Christians who are ready to witness for Christ have an easier time defeating the evil one.

Faith – Satan is the source and planter of unbelief and doubt. *"Has God said?"* is his favorite approach (see Genesis 3:1). *Faith* is what overcomes every foe (see 1 John 5:4). As believers use the *shield of faith, the fiery darts of unbelief, and doubt are kept away from them.*

Salvation – verse 17 is probably speaking about our ultimate *salvation* when Christ returns (see 1 Thessalonians 5:8). The believer whose *mind is fixed* on Christ's *imminent return* will not fall into Satan's traps and deceptions. The *blessed hope* must be like a *helmet to protect the believer's head and mind.* The head, of course, was the core of a soldier's *power to wage war.* His thinking ability was the most important factor in determining his victory or defeat. Therefore, the sign of the Christian soldier is the *helmet of salvation (deliverance).* He must protect his mind and its thoughts, keeping all thoughts focused on the Leader, *the Lord Jesus Christ,* and His objective of reaching the world with the *glorious news* that men could live forever.

The helmet that protects the mind of the Christian soldier is *salvation*. Unless a person has been saved, his or her mind cannot be protected from the *fiery darts of temptation*. The mind of an unsaved person is focused upon this world (earth); it is normal and natural for him or her ...

- to seek more and more
- to possess more and more
- to look at the opposite sex with desire
- to taste and indulge the good things of the earth
- to feel and experience, satisfying his or her desires and passions
- to have and hoard even when others have little or nothing

The unsaved person sees nothing wrong with being his or her own person and doing their own thing just so they are reasonably considerate of others. His or her mind and thoughts are upon the world; and the fiery darts of extravagance, indulgence, pleasure, self-centeredness, worldliness, license, hoarding, and immorality are a part of the unsaved world's daily behavior.

But this is not so with the saved person. The mind of the saved person is focused upon *Christ and mission* of sharing the good news of life, both life abundant and life eternal. Because of this Satan launches his fiery darts of temptation against the mind of the believer, trying to get his or her thoughts and attention off of Christ and the conquest and ministry to souls. The Christian soldier desperately needs the helmet of salvation. The *helmet of salvation* means the knowledge and hope of salvation. Knowing that we are saved and hoping for the glorious day of redemption:

- stirs us to keep our minds and thoughts upon Christ instead of on sin and this world.
- arouses us to focus upon Christ and His mission to carry the gospel to a needy and dying world.

Satan would love to have us believe that Christ is not coming back, or that He may not return today. Carefully read (Matthew 24:45-51) to see what the person who takes off the *helmet of salvation* looks like.

The Scripture distinctly points out that these pieces of armor are for the believer's *protection*. The *sword and prayer* are offensive weapons for attacking Satan's strongholds and defeating him. The Christian must fight spiritual enemies with spiritual weapons. (see 2 Corinthians 10:4), and the Word of God is the *only sword we need.* God's sword has *life* and *power* and never grows dull. *"For the word of God is quick and powerful, and sharper than any two-edged, sword, piercing even to the dividing asunder of soul and spirit, and of joints and marrow, and is a discerner of the thoughts and intents of the heart"* (Hebrews 4:12 KJV). Christians are conquering as they understand God's Word, memorize it, and obey it.

THE POWER WE EXERT (6:18-24)

Armor is not enough to win a battle; there must be *power* to get the job done. Our power comes from *prayer.* We use the sword of the Spirit, and we pray in the Spirit: the Holy Spirit *empowers us* to win the battle. Prayerfully read again Ephesians 3:14-21 and believe it with all your heart. The Word of God and prayer are the *two resources* God has given the church to overcome Satan and open territory for God's glory. Please note Acts 20:32 and Acts 6:4 also 1 Samuel 12:23.

LITTLE PRAYER YEILDS LITTLE POWER – MUCH PRAYER YIELDS MUCH POWER!

Christian soldier must pray with their eyes open. *"watch and pray"* is God's secret for overcoming the *world* (Mark 14:38), the *flesh* (Mark 14:38), and the *devil* (Ephesians 6:18). We should also "watch and pray" for opportunities to serve Christ (Colossians 4:2-3). We should not only pray for ourselves, but we should also pray for our fellow soldiers (6:19).

Paul was never too proud to ask for prayer. He wanted to have the *power* to be able to share the mystery (see 3:1-12), the very message that brought him to jail. *"Ambassador in bonds,"* a particular title, yet that is exactly what Paul was. Chained to a different Roman soldier every six hours, Paul had a wonderful opportunity to witness for Christ.

He closes this great epistle with several personal notes: 1. He knew his friends would want to know his condition. 2. They could pray for him if they knew his needs. Paul wanted to comfort them (v.22). 3. Paul was a true saint, drawing upon God's supply for his every need.

STUDY GUIDE FOR CHAPTER 16
WALKING IN VICTORY

1. Sadly many believers don't know the _____ God has made for _____ over Satan.

2. Just as the Spirit of God works in the believer – Satan and his demons work in the lives of unbelievers.

3. It is foolish to fight _____ and _____ when the real enemy is merely using flesh and blood to _____ the Lord's work.

4. The only way to fight spiritual enemies is with the Word of God and prayer.

5. The believer whose mind is fixed on Christ's imminent return will not fall into Satan's traps and deceptions.

6. The sword and prayer are offensive weapons for attacking Satan's strongholds and defeating him.

7. "Watch and pray" is God's secret for overcoming the world (see Mark 14:38, The flesh (Mark 14:38), and the devil (Ephesians 6:18).

CHAPTER SEVENTEEN

The Christian Soldier's Charge!

"Seek the LORD and his strength, seek his face continually" (1 Chronicles 16:11).

The Christian soldier enters the battle fully dressed and armed, but something else is essential: great confidence and courage. Such comes from a spirit of prayer.

The following things need to be noted about the soldier's prayer:

1. The soldier must pray – always pray. The soldier who is not always praying is not assured of God's protection. The Christian soldier must pray all the time to *maintain* a constant unbroken consciousness of God's presence and care. Prayer infuses the needed assurance, confidence, and courage.

"Seek the LORD and his strength, seek his face continually" (1 Chr. 16:11).

---

2. The soldier must pray "in the Spirit," that is, the Holy Spirit, the /spirit of the only living and true God. Prayer to any other god or to one's own thoughts or to some other man-made *god* is empty and useless.

"Likewise the Spirit also helpeth our infirmities: for we know not what we should pray for as we ought: but the Spirit itself maketh intercession for us with groanings which cannot be uttered. And he that searcheth the hearts knoweth what is the mind of the Spirit, because he maketh intercession for the saints according to the will of God" (Romans 8:26-27 KJV).

3. The soldier must be *sleepless in prayer*. The Christian soldier must concentrate and persevere in prayer. He must go to the point of being *sleepless* in prayer – sometimes so intensely involved in prayer that he actually goes without sleep in order to pray.

"Watch and pray, that ye enter not into temptation: the spirit indeed is willing, but the flesh is weak" (Matthew 26:41 KJV).

4. The soldier must pray unselfishly. The soldier is not in battle alone; many are engaged in the same warfare. The outcome of the battle is determined by the welfare of all involved. The Christian soldier must pray for those who fight with him. The Christian soldier must pray as much and, as intensely for his fellow soldiers as for himself.

"Wherefore I also, after I heard of your faith in the Lord Jesus, and love unto all the saints, cease not to give thanks for you, making mention of you in my prayers" (Ephesians 1:15-16 KJV).

5. He must pray for leaders in particular. Leaders, their decisions and example, often determine the outcome of the battle. The Christian soldier has leaders who teach, preach, and administer throughout the church and around the world. Boldness and decisiveness and purity are needed to put the enemy to flight and to capture souls for the gospel (see Acts 28:20).

"Now I beseech you, brethren, for the Lord Jesus, and for the love of the Spirit, that ye strive together with me in your prayers to God for me" (Romans 15:30 KJV). "Finally, brethren, pray for us, that the word of the Lord may have free course, and Be glorified, even as it is with you" (2 Th. 3:1 KJV).

TWO EXAMPLES OF CHRISTIAN SOLDIERS (6:21-24)

This passage presents two Christian soldiers, who were faithful to the Lord Jesus Christ. They are dynamic examples for every person who has enlisted in the great army of the Lord.

TYCHICUS (vv. 21-22)

Paul says three significant things in these verses about this great soldier of Christ.

1. He was a beloved brother – a man who believed in Jesus Christ and demonstrated it by his deep love for others. He treated others as brothers and sisters, loving and helping them as he could. Therefore, others counted as dear to their hearts, as a belove brother. (also see Acts 20:35; Galatians 6:10).
2. He was a faithful minister – a man called and gifted by God to preach the gospel and to minister to the needs of God's people. He had a world-wide vision; and he gave his life to reach people of the world with the glorious news that living forever was now possible. And note he was faithful. There was no slack or routine, or complacency, or weakening; he did not fail in his ministry. He

was a faithful minister – faithful in the Lord. He knew where his strength came from, and he drew his strength from the Lord daily. (see also John 9:4; Acts 4:20).

3. He was a friend of believers – a messenger of encouragement. Paul was in prison. The believers far off Ephesus were concerned about his welfare, and Paul was concerned that they know he was doing well through the strength of the Lord. How? Tychicus had his own ministry. He could have been preaching and teaching anywhere in the world. Yet here he was giving his time and energy to helping Paul and serving in Paul's ministry. He is seen giving up a separate ministry in order to serve as a dear friend and fellow minister with Paul. Apparently, he was the ideal minister and messenger of encouragement.

PAUL (vv. 23-24)

1. A glimpse into the heart of Paul can be reaped from these two verses. He was a spiritual brother to other believers. Notice, his concern was for the spiritual welfare of others:
   - He wished for them to have *peace:* security, harmony, freedom from disturbance.
   - He wished for them to have *love:* tenderness, warmth, and devotion.
   - He wished for them to have *faith:* belief and trust, loyalty.

2. Paul was a prayer warrior for other believers. He prayed that God's *grace* would rest upon them.

3. As a Christian soldier, your mission may be long, hard, and unheralded. But at all times the grace of God is there to see you through. As you serve day by day, you are above all else, to be concerned about the spiritual welfare of others and be a prayer warrior for other believers.

When we tire of our roles and responsibilities, it helps to remember God has planted us in a certain place and told us to be a good accountant or teacher or mother or father. Christ expects us to be faithful where He puts us, and when He returns, we'll rule together with Him.

STUDY GUIDE: CHAPTER 17
THE CHRISTIAN SOLDIER'S CHARGE

1. The Christian soldier who is not always praying is not assured of God's protection.

2. "Watch and pray that ye _____ not into_____ ..."

3. The Christian soldier must pray as much and as intensely for his or her _____ _____ as for _____.

4. He or she must pray for leaders in particular.

5. Boldness, and decisiveness and purity are needed to put the enemy to flight and to capture souls for the gospel (see Acts 28:20).

6. The passage presents two soldiers _____ and _____ who were faithful to the Lord's service.

7. When we tire of our roles and responsibilities, it helps to remember God has planted us in a certain place and told us to be a good accountant or teacher, or mother or father. Christ expects us to be faithful where He puts us, and when He returns, we'll rule together with Him.

CHAPTER EIGHTEEN

The Wiles, Devices, And Deceptions Of The Devil

Paul describes this weaponry as "the whole armor of God." Please note, the phrase "of God." This phrase is taken from the Greek phrase *tou Theo and* written in the genitive case – which simply means our supernatural set of weaponry *comes directly from God.*

God Himself is the *Source* of origin for the armor. Just as we draw our life, our new nature, and our spiritual power from God, the spiritual armor also comes from God as well. **This is important:** When a believer temporarily ceases to walk in fellowship with and in the power of God, he or she is *choosing* to temporarily step away from the *Source* from which their armor comes. When one makes this choice not to walk in fellowship with the Lord, in that condition, they no longer enjoy abundant life as they once did.

While abundant life still belongs to you, this state of stagnation will pull the plug on your spiritual walk – allowing the abundant life you once enjoyed to drain away until you eventually feel empty inside.

Why? Because abundant life has its source in the Lord. Additionally, that believer no longer enjoy the operation of God's power in their life.

Furthermore, the believer's ability to walk in his or her spiritual armor when their fellowship with the Lord has been suspended. Praise God, the believer's spiritual armor is still available for him to use and enjoy. But because he or she has suspended their fellowship with the Lord. Therefore, that believer has also opted to temporarily suspend his or her ability to walk in the armor of God. The very armor God gave to protect them. Why?

Because spiritual armor has its origin in the Lord. Whenever you put your spiritual life temporarily "on hold," you are opting to lay aside your spiritual armor. And you will only be able to pick up your armor again when you repent and begin to walk in right fellowship with the Lord once again.

THE ARMOR OF GOD IS OURS BY VIRTUE OF OUR RELATIONSHIP WITH GOD!

This is the reason Paul wrote in the genitive case. He wanted us to know that this armor originates in God and is freely bestowed upon those who continually draw their life and existence from God.

YOUR UNBROKEN, ONGOING FELLOWSHIP WITH GOD IS YOU ABSOLUTE GUARANTEE THAT YOU ARE CONSTANTLY AND HABITUALLY DRESSED IN THE WHOLE ARMOR OF GOD.

In Ephesians 6:11, Paul says, "Put on the whole armor of God ..." God has provided the complete outfit for us, not just a partial one. Like the Roman soldier, everything needed to successfully combat his adversary was available for him. So it is with the believer, God has given us everything we need to successfully combat *opposing spiritual forces. Nothing lacking!*

Sadly, it is unfortunate that some denominations and other organizations have majored only on certain parts of the armor of God.

Some teach heartily on the "shield of faith" and the "sword of the Spirit" while neglecting the other pieces of armor God has given believers. We are commanded to put on the *WHOLE* armor of God:

1. The belt of *truth*
2. The breastplate of *righteousness*
3. The shoes of *peace*
4. The shield of *faith*
5. The helmet of *salvation*
6. The sword of the *Spirit*

Paul commands us to pick up this complete set of spiritual weaponry and use continually throughout our Christian lives.

THE BATTLEFIELD OF YOUR LIFE AND MIND

As Paul continues in this passage, he tells *why* we need this armor. He says, "Put on the whole armor of God, *that you may be able to **stand** against the wiles of the devil.*" We pay attention to the phrase "... *that you may be able ...*" The word "able" is derived for the word *dunamis,* and it describes *explosive ability* and *dynamic strength or power.* Using this word *dunamis,* Paul declares that when we are equipped with the whole armor of God, we have explosive and dynamic power at our command. That is why He goes on to say, *"that you may be able to **stand against** ...."* Here he presents the picture of a Roman soldier who is standing tall and upright with his shoulders back and his head lifted up (a proud and confident soldier).

Paul uses the Greek word *stenia,* and it literally means *to stand.* The word *stenia* depicts what we look like in the **spirit realm** when we are walking in the whole armor of God. This word *stenia* was used in a military sense, meaning to stand your ground (position) on the battlefield.

This is important, for you have a responsibility to *stand guard over your mind.* Spiritual warfare is primarily *a matter of the mind.* As long as the mind is held in check and is *renewed to right thinking by the word of God, the majority of spiritual attacks will fail.* In doing so, you are actually placing a guard around every other battlefield in your life!

If God has called you to fulfill a specific assignment in the Body of Christ, you must stand guard over your position until it is completed.

The devil does not want you to fulfill the call of God on your life, so he will try to attack that divine call and turn it into a battlefield. So, until the job is completed, and the battle is won, you must stand guard over the will of God for your life. You must determine that you will not give the enemy an inch. This is your responsibility!

STANDING AGAINST THE WILES OF THE DEVIL

The question may come up, why do we need this armor? Paul tells us: "Put on the whole armor of God, that you may be able to stand against *the wiles of the devil"* (Ephesians 6:11). Then, what are the wiles? In his book, *Dressed to Kill,* Rick Renner explains the word "wiles" is one of three key words you must know and understand when studying the subject of spiritual warfare. The other two words are *devices* and *deception.*

The word "wiles" is taken from the Greek word *methodos.* It is a compound of the words *meta* and *odos.* The word meta is a preposition that simply means *with.* The word *odos* is the Greek word for *a road.* Compounded together, they form the word *methodos;* which literally translated, means *with a road.[19]*

The word "wiles" (*methodos*) often translated to something that is *cunning, crafty, subtle, and deception.* However, the most basic translation of the word is its literal meaning *with a road.[20]* Believe it or not, the devil does not have a bag of tricks. The word "wiles" (methodos) plainly means that the enemy has one "road" he travels; that is one trick in his bag. Where is the devil's road going? We find out in our second word (devices).

WE ARE NOT IGNORANT OF SATAN'S *DEVICES*

The word "devices" is derived from the Greek word *nous,* which depicts the hideous plots, and wicked schemes Satan (the devil) deploys to attack and victimize the *human mind.* One expositor has defined the "devices" as *mind games.* The idea of the word Paul uses in II Corinthians 2:11, gives the idea of a **deceived mind.**

---

[19]   Rick Renner, *Dressed to Kill* (Teach All Nations, a division of Rick Renner Ministries, published by Harrison House, Tulsa, OK, 1991) 196

[20]   Ibid. 197

Paul used the word *"devices"* to describe attacks that he had personally resisted, so we know that even he had to deal with Satan's *mental assaults* from time to time. Paul knew from experience about the *mind games* the devil tries to pull on people. It was for this reason that Paul said,

> *"Casting down imaginations, and every high thing that exalteth itself against the knowledge of God and bringing into captivity every thought to the obedience of Christ."* (2 Corinthians 10:5 KJV)

Satin loves to make a playground out of people's minds!

He loves to fill their emotions and senses with illusions that captivate their minds and ultimately *destroy* them. Like Paul, we must make a mental decision to take charge of our minds, *"… bringing into captivity every thought to the obedience of Christ."* It is a known fact, whoever a person's mind also controls that person's health and emotions. Knowing this, the devil seeks to penetrate a person's intellect (mental control center) and flood it with deception and falsehood. Once this is accomplished, the devil can then begin to manipulate that person's body and emotions – from a position of control.

Once Satan succeeds in penetrating and building a road into a person's mind, and emotions, the process of mental and spiritual captivity in that person's life is set. What takes place next is up to the one being attacked:

1. He or she can throw out this satanic process by renewing their mind with the Word of God.
2. And by allowing God's power, the Holy Spirit to do the work within them.

However, If the person does not choose to renew his or her mind and yield to the work of the Holy Spirit, it will be only a matter of time before a strong stronghold of deception begins to dominate and manipulate the person's self-image, emotional status and overall thinking – opening the door wider for the devil's deception.

THE DEVIL'S DECEPTION

Deception happens when someone believes the lies that the enemy has been telling them. Once a person begins to accept Satan's allegations is the very moment those wicked thoughts and mind games begin to produce Satan's reality in his or her life.

For example, the devil may attack your mind by repeatedly telling you that you are a failure. However, as long as you (both in their full armor) resist those demonic allegations, they will have no power in your life. But if you begin to agree with these lies and to mentally perceive them as the truth. Those lies will begin to control you and dominate your emotions and thinking. And finally your faith in those lies will give power to them and will cause them to create a false reality in your life – *and you will become a failure*. Here manifested is completed deception.

So many marriages fail because of false allegations that the devil tries to pound into the minds of each spouse. Remember! As long as the couple *repels* these allegations, Satan's lies exert no power in the marriage. However, if one of the spouses begins to entertain and dwell on these lies, he or she has crossed the first boundary line to a fatal deception.

In the beginning both spouses are absolutely aware that these suspicions are outright lies of the enemy. He or she thinks their marriage is the best ever. Meantime the enemy continues to pound away on this spouse's mind:

- Your wife [or husband] isn't pleased with you.
- Your marriage is really on the rocks.
- Your relationship can never last.

Unfortunately, this Christian continues to entertain these lying insinuations, the door remains open for the devil to continue to pound away at that person's mind and prey upon his or her emotions. Sometime later, the person's mind, battered and weary from worry begins to believe those false allegations. That spouse's faith in these lying emotions and suspicions can then empower the lies to become a reality in his or her marriage.

By mentally embracing these false insinuations, this spouse opens the door for the enemy to penetrate his or her mind. Thus, the process of confusion is executed; mind games are set in motion and that believer's perception of things become twisted. Unless this seducing process is not stopped at this point, in a matter of time the weary-minded believer begins to embrace these *mental lies* as though they were really the truth.

When a believer believes that their marriage is over, that they will die of terminal cancer, or that all hope for the future is gone, they are opening the door for the enemy to move these lying suggestions from the thought realm to the natural realm, where they become reality. These false perceptions empower the lies, giving the devil space to use these false beliefs to create his chaos in the natural realm.

When you engage in the devil's mind games, and perceive them s truth, you give power to them!

You must take charge of your mind and begin to speak God's truth to yourself to counter the devil's lies, otherwise the complete process of deception will continue to work in your life. Eventually, your greatest fears will become reality.

I pray that you can see now why these three words — the *wiles, devices,* and *deceptions* of Satan are so important for us to thoroughly understand, when studying spiritual warfare. This is why we must deal with the flesh before we attempt to deal with the devil. By living a crucified, and sanctified life on a continual basis, we are able to neutralize any attack the enemy would try to mount against our flesh.

Hopefully, you now understand the urgent command of Paul in Ephesians 6:11. If you are going to live free of Satan's lies and accusations, it is imperative that you *"Put on the whole armor of God – the lionbelt, breastplate, shoes, shield, helmet, sword, and lance; that comes from God, that you may have explosive and dynamic power to stand upright, against the roads that the devil would try to pave into your mind.*

ADVERSARY

Some people think the devil is what old folk use to call, a "play pretty." It is imperative that all Christians come to the realization that the devil is not just passively opposed to the presence of righteousness or righteous people. He is actively pursuing them and doing all within his power to wipe them out! He tries to devour us with present temptations or with past memories. In so doing, he tries to assault our sense of righteousness. This is why Peter said, "Be sober, be vigilant, because your adversary the devil, as a roaring lion, walketh about seeking whom he may devour." (1 Peter 5:8 KJV)

However, in the case of the devil, his roar is more fearsome than his bite.

Colossians 2:15 victoriously declares, "And having spoiled principalities, and powers, He (Jesus) made a show of them openly, triumphing over them in it"

By means of the Cross and the resurrection, Jesus Christ stripped these demonic powers bare of the authority they once possessed. Jesus' victory over them was so thorough that He even "made a show of them openly." Glory to God!

STUDY GUIIDE: CHAPTER 18 THE WILES, DEVICES, AND DECEPTIONS OF THE DEVIL

1. Just as we draw our life, our new nature, and our spiritual power from God, He is also the _____ from which our armor comes.

2. When one makes the choice to no longer walk in fellowship with the Lord, in that condition, they no longer enjoy _____ _____ as they once did.

3. Paul commands us to pick up the complete set of spiritual armor and _____ it _____ throughout our Christian lives.

4. Paul declares that when we are equipped with the whole armor of God, we have _____ and _____ .

5. It is important for you have a responsibility to stand guard over your mind! As long as the mind is held in check and is _____ to right thinking by the _____ of _____.

6. Spiritual warfare is primarily a matter of the mind.

7. Once Satan succeeds in penetrating and building a road into a person's mind, and emotions, the process of mental and spiritual _____ in that person's life. What takes place next is up to the person _____ _____.

A FINAL WORD

THE POWER OF THE GOSPEL

In order to be popular and accepted by the culture, or even to do good in the culture, it is expected of modern Christians to forget or downplay the gospel, the power behind everything we do. This gospel only works as power if God is truly both transcendent and personal, and He can only be that if He is the Trinity. The god news of God's love depends on this mysterious doctrine.

Only love will *powerfully move* our sin-sick souls as we come to understand the truth of both God's genuine personhood and his condescension. The Apostle John says, "See what kind of love the Father has given to us, that we should be called the children of God; and so we are." (1 John 3:1). This is the message of the Bible in its entirety, God condescension or self-abasement to reach sinful creatures. "For thus says the One who is high and lifted up, who inhabits eternity, whose name is Holy: I dwell in the high and holy place, and also with him who is of a contrite and lowly spirit, to revive the spirit of the lowly and to revive the heart of the contrite." (Isaiah 57:15). It is God by His Spirit who empowers the *preaching of the gospel* to bring rebellious human hearts to conviction of sin and to show them the need of a loving Savior.

THE GOSPEL IS GOOD NEWS

The Gospel is good news because there is bad news. Part of the mystery of God's person is His necessary function as moral Source and final Judge. In his introduction of the gospel, the Apostle Paul exhorts, "that the wrath of God is revealed from heaven against all ungodliness and unrighteousness of men, who by their unrighteousness suppress the truth." (Romans 1:18)

You may have been shaken a bit at the mention of wrath. The very idea of wrath in human beings implies out-of-control anger. However, God's wrath is never out of control, and its purpose is to assure us that we live in a moral universe with moral accountability. The gospel depends on this. It is part of Jesus' teaching; He states, "I came to cast fire on the earth, and would that it was already kindled! I have a baptism to be baptized with [death on the cross], and how great is My distress until it is accomplished! Do you think that I have come to give peace on earth? No, I tell you, but rather division" (Luke 12:49-51).

For there to be good news, undoubtedly there must be bad news. Human beings are by nature (Adam's) sinners and need to be made aware of this as Jesus has said. The level of sin can and does grow worse as we are experiencing today. In fact, at certain points, God as judge must act as judge within history.

GOD GAVE THEM OVER

In Romans 1, the text declares three times that God gave over sinners to the effects of their sin:

- "God gave over sinners to the lusts of their hearts" (Romans 1:24)
- God gave over sinners to dishonorable passions" and to "a debased mind" (Romans 1:26, 28)
- God "gives over" sinners, who, at a deep level, exchange the Truth for the Lie.

This act of God, the righteous Judge, in giving them over means "His abandonment of the persons concerned to more intensified and gross cultivation of the lusts of their own hearts which results in the receiving for themselves [in this life] a correspondingly greater amount of retributive judgment. Therefore, this action of God within history is an anticipation of God's final judgment, when it will be too late for mercy (see Romans 2:6-10). Yet it is also an occasion for hope, for seeing our sin can bring us to Christ.

Even though now we see our culture's blatancy in disregard for truth – as clearly presented in nature, His Word, and His Son – which may very well lead to God "giving over" those who resist Him in unbelief.

Our culture is putting much pressure on Christian pastors and teachers to avoid preaching and teaching the full extent of Romans 1. But covering up sin and denying the fall by refusing to reflect the Bible's position on homosexuality and other sins will only conceal and silence the liberating power of the glorious gospel.

GIVEN OVER BUT NOT GIVING UP

To hear the good news we must hear the bad. How can we deny the world the best news it could ever hear? "God did not spare His own Son but *gave Him over* for us all." How can we deny those we love the best news in the world? We must preach the gospel, even if doing so gives us over to persecution or even death. We will not give up.

Do you long for true spiritual power? You can have this justifying power from guilt and sin and the free conscience found when we discover and receive faith in Jesus Christ. In consenting to being given over, Jesus did not give up, and three days later God raised Him from the dead. So the gospel is all about God's work: the forgiveness of our sins and a future resurrected with Him. The same message that the early church preached is the one we now carry forward by the Spirit of God – For His Glory!

A CHARGE TO KEEP I HAVE

Printed in the United States
by Baker & Taylor Publisher Services